The wonder of
WOOLIES

The wonder of WOOLIES

**Memories from both sides of the counter of
Britain's best-loved store**

Compiled by

DEREK PHILLIPS

with a foreword by **Paul Atterbury** of the
Antiques Roadshow

CHAPLIN BOOKS

www.chaplinbooks.co.uk

First published in 2009 by Footplate Publishing, a forerunner of Chaplin Books
Copyright Derek Phillips

ISBN 978-0-9553334-5-3

A CIP catalogue record is available for this book from
The British Library

Consulting editor Dr Amanda J Field
Design by Helen Taylor
Printed in the UK by Imprint Digital

Chaplin Books
1 Eliza Place
Gosport PO12 4UN
Tel: 023 9252 9020
www.chaplinbooks.co.uk

WOOLWORTH'S – A TRIBUTE

You were on our high streets,
In our towns and cities;
You were there for us,
Whether rich or poor,
Through the war years,
In good times and bad.

Now, as you pass into history,
A comforting presence has gone
And the high street echoes with memories.
Perhaps a future generation
Will read about you
And come to understand
Why Woolworth's will always be
That great iconic store.

Pamela Phillips

CONTENTS

FOREWORD

by Paul Atterbury of the *Antiques Roadshow*

I grew up in the 1950s in Westerham, a small town in west Kent. It was a pleasant place, typical of its time and enjoyed a certain fame through its associations with General Wolfe and Sir Winston Churchill. Like all such towns, it was self-contained and self-sufficient. The main street was lined with independent shops of every kind, the owners of which were generally well-known and friendly. There was a toyshop, a bookshop and a big shop selling stationery: as a small boy, these spanned the limits of my interest.

We had a couple of national names, Boots and Cullens, but even these shops seemed essentially local. It was a regular treat, therefore, to visit bigger towns nearby, usually by bus, and to come into contact with a wider world. The highlight for me of such visits was the sight of the distinctive red façade of Woolworth's. This was truly a wonderful place, filled with an unbelievable variety of temptations. It was a shop of astonishing diversity and I could never tire of wandering up and down its colourful aisles. The nearest branch was quite small but outings to grandparents brought me into contact with much larger ones, such as Kingston-on-Thames.

And occasionally, as I grew older, my grandmother took me on day trips to London, trips that usually included visits to a Lyons Corner House and a major branch of Woolworth's, the size and richness of which simply took my breath away.

My interests then were focussed on sweets, toys and games but as I grew older my horizons opened out, taking in clothes and shoes, fishing equipment, tools and paint, magazines and gramophone records. Like many people of my generation, I simply took Woolworth's for granted.

It was always there, always somewhere that would have that odd thing I was looking for. The decades rolled by but somehow it survived, always looking much the same. It was just a fixed point in the high street, a comforting certainty in every part of Britain, the chain store where everyone felt at home.

From the 1970s the high street began to change. Local shops vanished, replaced by an ever-increasing variety of national names and big brands, and bit by bit every town in Britain came to look the same. In the midst of all this flashy sameness, Woolworth's came to represent traditional values and local interests, an irony as it was actually one of the first national, even international, names to enter our streets.

There were changes in style and presentation as Woolworth's struggled to keep up to date and fight off the competition. There were changes in ownership and each new corporate owner promised to bring this valuable brand into the modern world. They all failed, inevitably, and their frantic efforts merely served to destroy that indefinable individuality that had made Woolworth's so distinctive, so successful and so loved, and thereby hastened its end. It was a tragedy when the name finally vanished from our streets but no-one was really surprised.

Everyone enjoys the occasional wallow in nostalgia and ever popular are old views of the villages, towns and cities of Britain, especially those that focus on the high street and its flanking shops.

There is an immediate sense of period, whether the view, often a postcard, shows the 1920s, the 1950s or the 1970s, a sense defined by cars and buses, by the clothes and hairstyles and above all by the shops. And in the centre of so many of these views, occupying a prime position in the high streets of Britain, and instantly recognisable, is Woolworth's, that fixed point in our memories and our experiences that helped to define shopping in the twentieth century.

This book, with its remarkable collection of memories and photographs, celebrates those experiences, and commemorates a name that was at the heart of family life for so many decades.

Paul Atterbury

Outside Woolworth's in Chertsey High Street, London, on New Year's Eve 1945

INTRODUCTION

The announcement in 2008 that Woolworth's, one of the longest-established and most respected retail chains of all time was going into administration – with every shop closing and every member of staff being made redundant – came as a real shock. The British economy was already reeling from the collapse of banks and other financial institutions, the 'credit crunch' that followed in its wake, and the loss of tens of thousands of homes and jobs. The sparkle of Woolworth's had undoubtedly dimmed in recent years, but somehow we thought it would always be there, a 'marker' in our high streets that was familiar not just to us, but to our parents, grandparents and great-grandparents too.

The departure of Woolworth's from our towns and cities featured nightly on television news programmes. Staff were shown close to tears, understandable because of the loss of their jobs with so little warning. What was extraordinary, perhaps, was that customers were close to tears too: there was a real sense that something had changed irrevocably, and not for the better. I am unable to think of any retail name whose demise has produced quite this reaction: it was as if people had received the news of the loss of an old friend with whom they had shared so many experiences. Just the fact that the shop had a nickname – 'Woolies' – speaks volumes about the affection in which people held it.

In the final days, the packed shelves emptied out as people fought over the last few items. Suddenly, the stark metal racking was revealed and it was a little like seeing through the trick at a magic show – the illusion that Woolies had sustained for so long had gone. Even the shelving itself was being stripped down and sold on the spot at knockdown prices, like stripping the carcass of a once-mighty animal.

In its later years, Woolworth's had been a shadow of its former self: still bright and brash but hardly a source of wonder. In its heyday, it was the place you went with your parents to buy buttons, dress material, shoelaces, lampshades, tin tacks, broken biscuits and paper chains. If you were good, you could persuade them over to the counters that sold lead soldiers, comics, peanuts and banana split toffee. Later you went with your friends, to loiter by the record counter and listen to the latest hits. It was always packed with crowds of eager shoppers jostling for the attention of the shop-girls behind the wooden counters, and claiming that they were next to be served.

In modernising, something of this old atmosphere was lost, though Frank Woolworth, the chain's founder, would have approved of the introduction of self-service, which had always been one of his aims. Personally I still found the stores inviting, and loved to wander around, even if I had no intention of buying anything – there was a bargain to be discovered. On holiday, whatever town we visited, we always seemed to head for Woolies, especially when our children were young, buying pick 'n' mix – situated temptingly just inside the doorway – or eating a fried breakfast in the upstairs cafeteria. It was something of a holiday tradition: as a boy in the late 1940s with my parents on our once-a-year trip to Weymouth, we bought sticks of peppermint rock. Naturally, Woolworth's had the cheapest in town.

The sight of empty shuttered Woolworth's shops in our high streets does little to lift the spirits. But dip into the pages of this book and you will find that Woolies is alive and well in people's memories. From both sides of the counter – staff and shoppers — and across several generations, the anecdotes abound. There are stories that will make you laugh, such as the one about the stockroom boys cleaning the floor with caustic soda, a solution that not only removed all the dirt, but also removed the stitching from their fashionable Teddy Boy shoes. There are a few stories that might well make you cry, too, such as when a sales girl was reprimanded for talking too long to a sailor while she was supposed to be serving: the sailor was her brother and he was lost at sea with his ship the very next day. Most of all, it is in the accompanying photographs – of proud employees lining up with their manager, or of a treasured ornament bought more than 40 years ago – that the true spirit of Woolies reveals itself.

Woolworth's – we salute you.

Derek Phillips

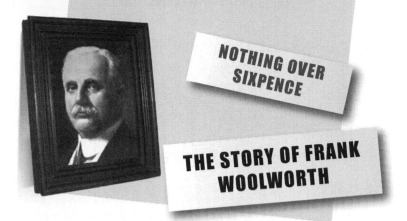

NOTHING OVER SIXPENCE

THE STORY OF FRANK WOOLWORTH

When Woolworth's first British store opened its doors at 2pm on Guy Fawkes day 1909, it seemed as if the whole of Liverpool had turned up to see what all the fuss was about. The opening ceremony had an air of grandeur, with two orchestras, fireworks and complimentary cups of tea. But the crush of shoppers, attracted by the penny, threepenny and sixpenny bargains, had to quell their enthusiasm – the first afternoon was strictly for 'browsing only.' The goods, according to the *Liverpool Courier*, 'occasioned the visitors considerable surprise in the matter of their exceptional value' and many thousand people returned the next day, eager to hand over their cash for everything from apple corers to cups and saucers. Though the *Daily Mail* thought Frank Woolworth's attitude to business resembled that of a Barnum-style circus proprietor rather than a shopkeeper, and were gloomy about the financial prospects, they could not have been more wrong. By the end of the first day's trading, the shelves were bare, staff were exhausted and every sweet in the shop had been sold. The wonder of Woolies had begun.

By the spring of 1910, Frank had two shops in Liverpool and had opened in Preston, Manchester, Leeds and Hull. It was just the beginning of an extraordinary expansion plan that would make Woolworth's a familiar site on almost every high street in the country: a part of the very fabric of life in Britain.

Woolworth's had begun in the US, where Frank Winfield Woolworth had earned the nickname 'king of the five and dime' for the success of his bargain-stores. Born on 13 April 1852 in

Picture: author's collection

King of the 'five and dime'– Frank Winfield Woolworth

Rodman, New York, a very different future had already been mapped out for him: once he'd finished school, he would work on his father's 108-acre farm, helping to look after eight dairy cows and tending the potato crops. But Frank had other ideas. At the age of 20, after four years on the farm, he volunteered to work without pay at the Augsburg and Moore dry-goods store in Watertown, New York, sweeping the floor and cleaning the shelves, so he could learn about merchandising. After three months, the store took him on as an employee. His career had begun, even if he had to work an 84-hour week for less than five cents an hour. Over the next six years, he worked his way up to the position of clerk, holding down a respectable salary of 10 dollars a week – enough to marry his Canadian girlfriend Jennie and settle down into family life.

In those days, all the goods in a store were on shelves or in cupboards behind the counter – the customer handed over a list to the sales clerk, who assembled the goods. Impulse buys were therefore unlikely. Frank watched with interest what happened when his employer held a clearance sale with left-over goods, setting them out on a table and marking them down to a dime (10 cents) or even to a nickel (5 cents). Though shoppers snapped up the bargains, the store-owner saw little potential in it. Frank had the glimmer of an idea: why not put all the goods out where the shoppers could pick them up themselves? In fact, why not have a shop that sold only five-cent goods?

Enthused, Frank Woolworth borrowed 300 dollars (£60) from his employer and opened his first five-cent store in Utica, New York on 22 February 1879 with another following in Lancaster, Pennsylvania, the oldest inland city in America. The Utica store failed after only four months, but Lancaster became a flourishing business: the world's first five- and ten-cent store. Best-selling items included tinware, toys, washbasins, towels, handkerchiefs and ribbons. Following his practice of thrift (or perhaps his pursuit of profit), Frank ensured that all goods were wrapped in newspaper, rather than wrapping paper, which would cost extra.

Frank signed up his brother Charles to manage his next store, in Scranton, Pennsylvania, which opened on 6 November 1880. By 1886 there were seven Woolworth's stores in operation, each displaying the carmine-red shop fronts, which in later years would be recognised worldwide. The famous diamond W trademark, also designed by Frank, appeared at this time.

For these early stores, Frank made his managers into partners and even rebranded some of the shops as Woolworth-Knox, in recognition of the partnership with his cousin, Seymour Knox. After running 12 stores in this way, Frank discontinued the practice in 1888: all the stores were to be in sole ownership, with the managers sharing the profits. The move meant Frank could pursue his own vision for the future of the business. He pioneered the practice of buying merchandise direct from the manufacturers rather than by haggling with wholesalers. His first visit to Europe, made in 1890, was on one of these buying trips: disembarking from the ship in Liverpool, he took a train to Stoke on Trent to purchase chinaware from the manufacturing potteries. He wrote in his diary: 'I think a good penny and sixpence store, run by a live Yankee would create a sensation here, but perhaps not.' It was to be nearly 20 years before he could find which of these speculations would prove true.

Frank's buying tour took him to Continental Europe, where he found in Germany a source of glass marbles at three cents per thousand, a highly favourable price compared with the 45 cents per thousand he was currently paying his US supplier. Christmas tree ornaments were another German bargain: Frank snapped up nearly a quarter of a million of them. He did not do things by halves.

When the number of Woolworth stores reached 120 in 1905, they were incorporated as F W Woolworth & Co, with Frank as president. The Corporation was now worth ten million dollars – a far cry from the day when the first store opened in 1879 with a loan of 300 dollars. Frank remembered his dream about taking Woolworth's to England, but met with a less than enthusiastic reaction from his managers. In fact the only people to reply to his offer to travel to the UK were two men who ran stores in New York City, Samuel Balfour and Frank's cousin Fred, plus a superintendent from Boston, Byron Miller. They set sail for England from Hoboken on the steamer Kaiserin Auguste Victoria on 19 May 1909.

The men made their base in London, using the railway system to travel the length and breadth of the country – as far north as Manchester and as far south as Southampton – in their search for suitable sites. British stores, in particular Harrods, did not impress them. On walking in, they were approached by the floorwalker who asked if he could assist them. Frank answered that they just wanted to look around: the floorwalker's attitude turned icy and he stalked away. 'Did you notice how he stared at us, as if we were a couple of muleskinners?' said Frank. 'He wouldn't last a week on my payroll.'

Though the men had travelled all around England, it was Liverpool, the port where they had disembarked from their steamer, that they chose for the first store. Liverpool had been dubbed the 'second city of the British Empire' and, as Frank clearly had an empire of his own in mind, it was an appropriate choice. The British arm of F W Woolworth & Co Ltd was formed with a capital of £50,000 and a lease was taken out on premises at the corners of Church Street and Williamson Street. Just four months was allowed for the installation of lighting, counters and fixings including a first floor tea-room.

The early years in the UK were not easy for the Woolworth

Corporation. On the opening day at Hull in 1910 the doors were proudly unlocked at 9am to admit one customer who ran the length of the counters, purchased a tin of brass polish and then ran out again. Not another customer was seen for two hours.

The opening of the second store in Liverpool at London Road was the scene of a near riot when hordes of barefoot women, known as the 'shawlies' due to their habit of wearing long shawls over their heads and shoulders, ran in and mobbed the counters. Pressure from the throng was so strong it pressed the mahogany counters against the walls causing the shop assistants to faint. During the melée, many of the 'customers' were plundering the counters and filling their shawls with as much as they could, and then running out of the store without paying as more crowds arrived intent on the same purpose.

The first Englishman to be employed by Frank was William Stephenson, who had been a young freight clerk in the Staffordshire potteries when Frank had made his buying trip to Europe. Stephenson had impressed the American entrepreneur – and Frank never forgot anyone who had helped him. He asked

Picture: author's collection

Woolworth's in Fore Street, Tiverton, Devon, in 1946. The fascia incorporates a '6d store' sign

Stephenson to move to Liverpool. 'Its no good asking about money,' said Frank. 'If we go bust, you're bust – if we make a do of it, I will look after you.' Stephenson agreed, and this was probably the wisest move he ever made. He stayed with Woolworth's throughout his working life, becoming chairman of the British operation in 1923 following the death of Fred Woolworth, and retaining the position for 25 years.

Frank's British managers, Fred Woolworth, William Stephenson and Byron Miller, put in 18-hour days getting new sites up and running, employing staff, ordering stock, accounting, and a myriad of tasks necessary for the creation of a new retail empire. They also had to learn to deal direct with manufacturers, just as Frank had done in the US, as the key to their retail success was buying goods in bulk, and cutting out the wholesalers.

By 1912 the British arm of Woolworth's was out of the red with 12 stores up and running. The American policy of using managers trained on their shop floor now operated within the British stores: a man (and in those days it was always a man) would

Picture: author's collection

High Street, Inverness, with Woolworth's on the left hand side, pictured in 1948 be employed in the stockroom and if he made the grade, would be promoted eventually to the position of manager. All Woolworth's managers and directors came up this way.

By now, in addition to his controlling interest in the British stores, Frank had 319 of his own shops operating in 27 American states. He decided to amalgamate these with the affiliated five-and-dime stores of his brother Sumner, his cousin Seymour Knox, E P Charlton, Fred Kirby and Willam Moore. The result was a corporation worth 65 million dollars, with 558 stores in the US, 32 in Canada and 12 in Britain. Woolworth's had 20,000 employees and served three million customers a day – all on a cash-only basis.

Frank smartened up his branding, dropping the ampersand from the name, now F W Woolworth and Co, and specifying that every storefront would be painted in the company's colours of

Picture: author's collection

Woolworth's in the 1960s: a prime position in Darley Street, Bradford

Queuing for the bus in the 1960s outside Woolworth's in Stowmarket

scarlet and gold. The next step was a corporate headquarters, something that Frank had long dreamed of. He commissioned architect Cass Gilbert to design an imposing 57-storey building in New York City on Broadway between Park Place and Barclay Street in Lower Manhattan. Upon completion in 1913 the Woolworth Building, constructed in neo-Gothic style, became the tallest habitable building in the world, a record it would hold until the construction of the Chrysler Building in 1930. At 792 feet (241 metres) it is still one of the 20 tallest buildings in New York City, and one of the 50 tallest buildings in the US, and is listed as a National Historic Landmark.

Faced with cream-coloured terracotta, the Woolworth building had an entrance arcade three storeys high with floors of marble terrazzo and marble walls rising to a vaulted dome ceiling studded with glass mosaic. The building used 24,000 tons of steel and 17,000,000 bricks in its construction, and all the doors, partitions and trims were made of steel, terracotta or wire glass – not just for modernity but for fire protection. There were 40 acres of floor area, 3,000 windows, 43 miles of plumbing pipes, 3,000 hollow-steel doors, 12 miles of marble trim, 28 elevators, 13,500 electrical sockets and 87 miles of electrical wiring. The 80,000 light bulbs, if strung out at one metre intervals, would have been sufficient to light a road stretching 40 miles around the waterfront of Manhattan Island. Frank Woolworth's magnificent office was a replica of Napoleon Bonaparte's Empire Room in the palace at Compiègne complete with wall panels of the finest marble.

At the opening banquet 900 invited guests watched the whole building being bathed in light as President Woodrow Wilson pressed a button in the White House to light up 80,000 light bulbs in the new Woolworth headquarters. The building had cost 13,500,000 dollars: Frank simply paid for it in cash.

The F W Woolworth Company occupied only one and a half floors of all this opulence: the rest was to be rented out, one of the first tenants being the Irving National Bank, of which Frank was a director.

Picture: Robert Parr/STTS Collection

Dumbarton Road, Partick, Glasgow on 4 August 1960: the tram just passing under the bridge is the number 16 service that ran between Scotstoun and Partick. The Woolworth's store can be seen on the left

By the start of the First World War, the company had 40 stores in Britain and Ireland: a total of 57 members of staff enlisted and sadly most of them were killed in action. Women managers were employed for the first time and more managers drafted in from the US.

Frank Woolworth died on 8 April 1919 just five days short of his 67th birthday. He had seen his company grow from a single store to a business worth 119 million dollars a year. He was succeeded by Hubert T Parson, who had been Frank's first bookkeeper, hired in 1892. Under Parson, the company continued to expand rapidly and from the mid-1920s was inundated with requests from councils throughout Britain asking for a store with its familiar scarlet frontage to be built in their town. At one point Parson was opening one new store every 17 days. By 1921 Mansfield in Nottinghamshire became the UK's one hundredth store.

In 1931 the British company was floated on the London Stock Exchange: within a few years the shares were paying dividends of

Picture: author's collection

The tram-stop outside the Woolworth's store in Leeds, around 1950

100 percent or more, making this one of the top ten British companies. The US banks had placed £5,000,000 at the disposal of the British company, but not a penny of it was touched. Cash-in-hand was the favoured way of doing business, and Woolworth's even abandoned the practice of taking out leases on premises: instead they bought the freehold.

Manufacturers were now queuing up to deal direct with the company with their policy of bulk buying and over the years, many of them would become household names. Ladybird, Matchbox, Dinky Toys, Airfix Kits and Chad Valley are just a few of the brands that owed their success to Woolworth's. The trading partnership with Ladybird began one day in 1932 when Woolworth's placed an order for 96,000 pairs of Directoire knickers from the firm, then called A Pasold & Son. Through Ladybird, Woolworth's came to control 6.5 percent of the children's clothing market and there would be very few children in the UK who did not at some time have items of clothing from the Ladybird range which also expanded into jewellery, pushchairs and bedding. Woolworth's bought the exclusive rights to the Ladybird name in 1984 and eventually purchased the company in 2000 from Coats Viyella for the sum of 11 million pounds. Even when Woolworth's collapsed, there was a ready buyer for the Ladybird brand, which was taken over by Shop Direct in January 2009.

As inflation took its toll, the five-and-dime policy in the US and the 'nothing over sixpence' in the UK had to go, though the stores still pursued the same bargain-hunter's market. They were quick to latch onto topical events and exploit the possibilities: Woolworth's became the top-selling retail chain for Festival of Britain memorabilia in 1951, and for the Coronation of HM Queen Elizabeth II in 1953, they launched a range of tablecloths, mugs, plates, gold crowns, flags and bunting. One particularly popular piece proved to be the model of the state coronation coach produced by Lesney Products. Launched in January 1953 a total of 500,000 were sold in 16 weeks and sales by the end of the year had reached one million, many of them sold over Woolworth's counters. The model is very collectable today. Model cars were a big hit for Woolworth's, thanks to a deal they struck with Lesney to supply the stores with Matchbox cars in boxes of 12 at a very good price.

By 1954 Woolworth's in Britain employed 50,000 people, ranging from shopgirls paid £4 a week through to managers earning the princely sum of £5,000 a year. Gross profits were soaring: in 1951 they topped £14 million, in 1952 they were £16 million and in 1953 they reached nearly £19 million. And as the post-war boom continued, Woolworth's went from 762 British stores in 1950 to 1,028 in 1959. It was a year of huge expansion: 16 new stores were opened (at Ashby, Bartley Green, Bo'ness, Cambuslang, East Kilbride, Edgeley, Forest Gate, Hatfield, Kenton, Kirkby, Kirkwall, Longbenton, Newtownards, New Washington, Shaw and West Heath) and a further 34 stores were modernised or extended (including Banbury, Basingstoke, Bexleyheath, Bolton, Burton on Trent, Consett, Cosham, Dunstable, Harlesden, Hastings, King's Lynn, Kingston, Leeds, Leigh, Manchester, Middleton, Mold, Nelson, Newry, Northampton, Pontypool, Redditch, Saltcoats, Strand, Sunderland, Swansea, Tooting, Tottenham, Wallasey, Waltham Cross, Wellington, Wimbledon, Winchester and

Picture: author's collection

The Woolworth's store at Gardiners Corner, Whitechapel, London, 1959

Woking). The 1950s also marked a major change in direction, with the introduction of self-service stores, the first opening in Cobham, Surrey.

The Winfield brand was launched in 1963 and the name was applied to everything from packets of buttons to sewing machines. All seemed to be going well: seeds of the impending crisis were not spotted until the 1970s but somehow Woolworth's had begun to lose its way. Pressure to modernise stores, and to fund the purchase of the B&Q chain of DIY outlets, led them to start closing their less successful shops: during the 1970s, 15 UK stores a year closed their doors. By the mid-1980s the Winfield brand had lost its popularity and was dropped. Woolworth's was feeling the competition both from other high street names, out-of-town stores and the huge product range available at hypermarkets and superstores. The American company announced it was going to sell its majority interest in the British stores, which were acquired by Paternoster Stores Ltd (forerunner to the Kingfisher Group) in 1982. The links to the American parent were now broken, but in fact the British stores would outlast their US counterparts. In 1997, the last 700 of Woolworth's US stores closed and the company changed its corporate name to Venator. It even moved out of the famous Woolworth building in 1999, changing names yet again – this time to Foot Locker, the corporation's top retail performer which sold athletic clothing and footwear.

The Woolworth's brand now only existed on the British high street. After a de-merger from the Kingfisher Group in 2001, Woolworth's Group plc was floated on the London Stock Exchange with shares priced at 32p. They peaked at 55p in 2005 before falling to a low of 15p by January 2008. On 26 November of the same year, Woolworth's announced that it was going into administration with the loss of 30,000 jobs and 815 stores. Many employees had given years of service to the company: the shock must have been immense. A rolling programme of closures began, with 200 stores at a time locking their doors. By 6 January 2009, Woolworth's had disappeared from Britain's high streets.

There have been some encouraging signs: Iceland, the frozen food retailer, bought 51 of the sites, and in Dorchester, Dorset,

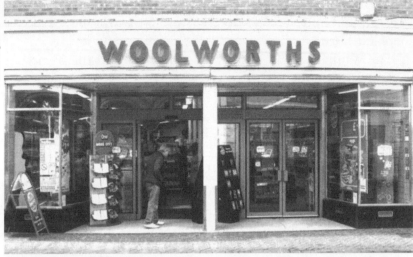

Picture: Roger F Newman

A plainer look: Woolworth's in Fore Street, Trowbridge in 2008

former Woolworth's manager Claire Robertson reopened her store under the name of 'Wellworths', employing 22 former members of staff, and attracting a blaze of publicity. The Woolworth brand name was bought by Shop Direct, the company that had earlier acquired the Ladybird brand, but the venture is an Internet-based one.

Strangely, the conditions that brought Woolworth's such success in the 1890s with its formula of supplying masses of cheap, quality goods, sold by staff attentive to the needs of the customer, are not so far different from those in 2009. In the 1890s, millions of impoverished immigrants were flocking into the US and had no choice other than to seek out the stores that offered goods they could afford. In 2009, the credit crunch, job losses and shorter working hours puts similar pressure on obtaining value for money. Although there are supermarket chains today who are very successful, it's doubtful that any of them will be remembered as fondly as Woolworth's and there is no doubt that if Frank Woolworth was alive today, then he would surely give them a run for their money.

Ballet shoes and overalls

'When I was 15 years old in 1953 I was faced with two serious employment options: a shop girl in Woolworth's or a glamorous career in the theatre. I was a curvy teenager, an attractive five foot nine inches tall with long wavy hair. I could kick my leg up as high as any Tiller girl and, boy, could I move. The choice was easy. I loved dancing but I was a home girl and loved family life in the South Wales valleys, so I joined Woolworth's at Abderdare. I remember my first day vividly. The staff supervisor put me to work in the grocery department. Instead of a dancer's slimming leotard I wore long, white overalls so thick and heavy they came down to my ankles. My shiny, bouncy hair was transformed into two dull bunches and decorated with a stiff, white, frilly upright headband with FWW embroidered on the front. I looked like a giant sanitary towel. Store rules dictated no jewellery and only a light dusting of make-up – quite different to modern-day department stores where it's de rigueur to be orange.

Woolworth's girls gave a personal 'over-the-counter' service to shoppers wanting everything from groceries and toiletries to stationery, hardware and toys. Mental arithmetic was imperative as we added each shopper's purchases up in our heads. Jotter pads, tied to our waists with a piece of string from the belt of our overalls, were reserved for multiple purchases only. The tills were exactly like the one used by Ronnie Barker in the TV show *Open All Hours* – big, brassy and noisy.

The store had no automatic lift. In order to replenish the counters, one of the stockroom boys would load up the lift, then stand inside the lift and pull on a thick cord. That was hard work. No health and safety executive or manual handling course to worry about. Every week we had to scrub the wooden shams and china tops, polish the glass and scour the floors. We worked diligently and extremely hard but I can only recall pleasant, frequently humorous memories.

After a very happy first year I was promoted from third girl in groceries to second girl on the sweet counter. Opposite me were the loose biscuits. Bliss! All kinds of sweets were sold by the pound and temptingly displayed in jars under glass counters. Bars of chocolate and tubes of sweets were laid out like soldiers, all facing the right way up, with brand names to the front, allowing the customer to choose in comfort. The distortion of heads and manipulation of necks required to browse the shelves of today's supermarkets would not have been tolerated in 1950s Woolies. Neither would the familiarity of addressing our colleagues by their first names. Mr Rivers, the store manager, would publicly reprimand all employees who either failed to display their wares in the appropriate manner or have the cheek to call a co-worker by anything other than their surname.

Eventually, the store was modernised and by the 1960s I had worked my way up to first girl and then supervisor in charge of six departments. Not bad for a lassie who left school with nothing but a pair of ballet shoes and a tutu. Not even marriage and the birth of three children could tempt me to leave Woolies and I worked part-time until the late 1970s.

My daughter loves to relate a story that today would result in a full investigation by social services and probably the removal of my children into emergency foster care. A few weeks after giving birth (I must have been suffering from some sort of sleep deprivation) I proudly pushed my long-awaited daughter in her giant-sized pram into town. For reasons of pure practicality, these magnificent baby transporters would line up just inside the doorway of Woolworth's: the aisles just would not have accommodated them while mothers shopped and gossiped at their leisure in the store. I parked my Susie alongside one or two others and off I went to buy ham, cheese, and anything else I fancied from the new delicatessen counter. I think I may have been dreaming of a piece of slab cake (sold by the pound). When I was walking home, I suddenly became aware that I was missing something. It wasn't my purse; that was still safe in my handbag. My two shopping bags seemed to contain everything I had bought; fruit and veg, fresh bread, tinned fruit cocktail. Why the funny feeling? I was almost home when I realised to my horror that I wasn't pushing the pram. With my heart in my mouth I ran all the way back to Woolworth's and there she was, baby Susie, in her protective cabin, still sleeping and still safe, just inside the doorway. No-one had noticed her mother had abandoned her and if they had, they would have kept an eye out until my return. I took a deep breath, pushed her home and had an extra large slice of cake with my cup of tea.'

Ruby Williams

One big happy family

'Although I passed my Eleven Plus, my parents could not afford to send me to the grammar school, so I started work at the age of 14. The headmaster had arranged an office job for me, but when I went to the interview I thought 'I could never work here.' Going up the high street in Market Harborough I saw the notice in Woolworth's window: 'Assistants required'. My parents were not pleased but it was the start of some happy years there, and a wage of 21 shillings a week.

Woolworth's was one big happy family: the manager was Miss Bennett, well-liked because she would put overalls on and work with the girls; and two really good supervisors, Miss Billington (Billy) and Minnie Palister who likewise worked with the girls. In the office was Kit Wadsworth and in the stockroom was Hilda Clarke. Along with us girls – I recall Maisie and Mary Cotton, Betty or Mary Whitbread, Amy Goodwin and Violet Bonner – it was a brilliant crowd.

On Thursdays we would go to the Pally at Leicester to the tea dance and often to all the local dances. At this time the Army and

Air Force were stationed in town so Woolworth's decided to open a tea bar, which became very popular. Mary Whitbread and myself went to Kettering to train for that: we had some great times on the tea bar.

As the years went by, the men started coming home from the forces, Miss Bennett moved to head office and we had a new manager come to the store. It was all change. The tea-bar closed and the atmosphere went with it – and so did I.'

Alma O'Brian

Biscuit delights

'All the counters at Market Harborough were wooden and each section had their own wooden till. The biscuits were displayed in silver tins: we had malted milk, nice, custard creams, fig rolls and digestives; some were also chocolate-coated. The biscuits were all sold loose by weight and could be mixed. There was a tin of broken biscuits, which were very popular as they were half price and we were also allowed to eat them'!

Lynda Buckingham

I thought I was rich

'When I first worked for Woolworth's in Ballymena, County Antrim, you had to start as a part-timer and work for a year before becoming eligible for full-time. I was there for 10 years, leaving in 1947 to emigrate to America.

We all stood behind counters in those days, with the goods displayed in front of us. Mr. Hanna was the manager: very strict, but very fair. You did not speak loudly to another assistant – you rang the bell and either Mr Hanna, or a supervisor came, and you gave your message to them. Mr Hanna was always standing at the front doors every morning and it was 'Good morning, Miss Buick', and so on. When we arrived and made our way to the office; we had to hand in our handbag to one of the office girls. You had to do this every time you wanted to leave or return. Also, if someone was waiting to be served, Mr Hanna looked around, snapped his fingers and you immediately gave your attention to the customer. When I left in 1947 the girls had a surprise lunch for me and Mr

Picture: Annie Field

Ballymena manager Tom Hanna and his staff gather to say goodbye to Annie Field as she emigrates to the US in 1947. Annie is third from left in the front row

Hanna asked Caulfield's (the shop next door) to deliver ice cream – a rare treat in those days. When I left my pay was two pounds 10 shillings per week, and I thought I was rich. We worked 9am – 6pm with a half-day on Wednesdays, but had to work until 9pm on Saturdays.'

Annie Field

All 10 fingers on the till

'I worked for the 'old style' Woolworth's here in Gallowtree Gate, Leicester for a couple of years in the late 1960s. At first I worked only on a Saturday on the counter selling hair curlers and combs. For this I wore a green overall with a narrow green band on my head.

Amazingly nothing was priced, so the prices had to be quickly learned, as customers would fill bowls with a mixture of hair rollers, hair nets, hair grips and so on. You had to be able to add the items up in your head.

After a few weeks I transferred to the meat counter upstairs. Now I wore a lemon coloured overall and hat and worked from

9.30am to 1.30pm and all day Saturday. This was a really busy area although the meat was all pre-packed. We were still responsible for keeping the counter clean, a nauseating job as some of the packaging leaked, especially at the end of the counter where the offal was displayed. We were not given any cleaning equipment apart from some dishcloths which, incidentally, were not washed. The adding-up went on the same, and so when the amount came to, say, a two-figure pounds, shillings, pence and halfpence sum, all 10 fingers had to be applied on the till and then the change reckoned.

Sometimes we were asked to help out on other counters, so I also served bacon, sausage, cooked meat and cheese, still in my blood-spattered overall. Thursday afternoon was early closing day, so in the morning the 'foreign' sausages such as salami, which hung on hooks over the counter, had to be taken down and coated with olive oil. A lot of ribald remarks were made over that! On the meat counter on a glass shelf were displayed tins of peas – they were still there when I left, unsold but well dusted! I was expecting a baby at this time, but was still allowed to work on the counter until I was seven months pregnant. After that I worked in the preparation room upstairs, weighing cooked meat into quarters, sandwiched between small squares of greaseproof paper. Usually this meant two slices of fresh ham, a slice of yesterday's unsold, then another fresh slice on top. I earned about £5 for the week, I believe.

I also worked on the biscuit and cake counter, where there was block cake which had to be cut and weighed as the customer requested. You can imagine how this had to be calculated, and the difference in density between Madeira cake, fruitcake and angel cake.

Another thing I remember was the tea-pouring in the canteen: the cups were laid out on an enamel tray with drainage holes, and the girl behind the counter would pour out several cups of tea without stopping, straight over the top of the cups. When I was a child I remember there was a very small area where people who just wanted a cup of tea (sometimes tramps) would sit on bar stools.

The work was hard but the other women were wonderful: some had worked there for years and I suppose most of us were working mothers trying to make ends meet at home.' *(Memories from a lady who forgot to put her name and address on her letter)*

Kitchen items? No thanks

'On leaving school, there was a choice of three jobs: office junior, nursing or shop work. There was no possibility of going to grammar school as I came from a very large family of nine children. Out of the three, I chose shop work when I left school at the age of 15 years in 1951.

I started at the High Street, Erdington, Birmingham branch of Woolworth's at £2 per week and was put on the plant counter selling bedding plants. I loved every day there and could not get to work quickly enough. I got on very well with my co-workers, managers and customers: it was a very happy place and I made a lot of friends. But when the season for bedding plants finished, I was transferred to soaps and kitchen items, which I didn't like one bit. It wasn't busy like my last counter. I tried for a few weeks to see if I could get on with the change, but couldn't, so I gave in my notice. They offered me a five shilling rise to stay but, though I tried really hard to like it, it was to no avail. After trying a few more jobs I ended up in catering, which I stayed in for the rest of my working life except for the years bringing up my children. I can truly say I loved working for Woolworth's.'

Jean Thacker

Glamorous colleagues

'When I started as an office junior at Fishponds, Bristol, in 1944, I discovered that my seat in the small office was the safe door pulled out with a cushion on the top. One of my jobs was to go into the shop and collect the takings twice a day from the tills. I loved to be in the shop: it was always so busy. Every girl on each counter ordered all her own stock, and most were very capable. The girls on the sweet counter always gave me lots of sweets and chocolate. I longed to be out in the shop and eventually wore down the manageress with my pleading. I was responsible for the counter selling ribbon and fancy goods and knew the stock and prices of everything I sold. Ration coupons were being used for sweets and bread at that time.

I have so many memories of that time watching some of the older girls (I was 14) in the rest room putting on their make-up.

Sybil, who worked on the sweet counter, was particularly glamorous. We got lots of American soldiers in the shop and some of the older girls went out with them – in fact a couple of girls married them and became GI Brides, eventually going to America to live. Some of the girls dated boys who wandered into the store on Saturdays and a few of us girls went to dances together in the evening.

I was sent on an exchange, to work at Woolworth's in Weston-Super-Mare for a week. Wow! What a week that was for a young girl.'

Janet Underhill

Life at the 'Flat'

'On leaving school at 15 in November 1953, I started work at Woolworth's in Hockley, Birmingham (a busy shopping centre known as the 'Flat'). I loved my job from day one and my weekly wage was three pounds five shillings. My first manager was Mr Hewitt, a middle-aged gentleman who was very strict and ran a tight ship. After a year on the haberdashery counter, I moved to the sweets and ice-creams counter, working with June Hodges who became my best friend. After that, I applied for the job of window dresser, and was sent to the window-dressing school at Woolworth's in the Bull Ring. When I'd completed my training I went back to my own store and my pay went up to four pounds ten shillings, which to me was a fortune. As time passed both my mother and aunt came to work with me: I had great friends in the store and there was a sense of good teamwork.

Mr Hewitt left our store to take a promotion at a larger store in Blackpool, and our new manager was a Mr Mountford, a younger man who was not as strict, which led to more of a relaxed atmosphere in the store. We enjoyed our jobs even more and the store flourished. After I married and started a family, we left England to start a new life in Australia, eventually returning to Birmingham in 1976. Whenever I pass the site in Hockley where the store used to be, my thoughts and memories are always very strong: I get quite emotional just thinking of all the girls I worked with there.'

Olive Holland

Seats weren't for sitting

'When I started working for Woolworth's at Chippenham in 1946, the stocks of soap, kilner jars, sweets and glass fruit sets were rationed. Customers had to queue for their purchases, which were priced in sections on the counters. Every Monday each person on his or her section had to remove everything off the counter and clean it. We had fold-up seats behind the counter but were not allowed to sit down or you could be fired. Our uniforms were supplied but the pockets had to be taken off in case anyone decided to pilfer anything.'

Ivy Dolman

'Fronting up' the paint display

'After being a Saturday girl at Woolworth's in Erdington, Birmingham, I went onto working more-or-less full time. I started off on the tills, when the rear of the shop used to have a centre till section. The home DIY section was behind it and I used to be responsible for filling up the shelves with tins of paint. I switched to working on the single-seat till located at the side door of the store, and moved to the cooked meat counter.'

Jane Murray

Phyl's word was law

'My mother Phyl worked in the stockroom at the Goring branch, west of Worthing, initially as a part-time assistant but later becoming full time and in charge. The Goring store was small and it was like a family. Everyone socialised and there were many parties and dinners. Phyl enjoyed the closeness of being 'one of the girls'. As her confidence grew at Goring, her word became law in the stockroom. The one thing she was not happy about was handling bananas, as spiders lurked within. She liked being a 'backroom' person and would not show her face on the shop floor if she could help it. She was the only person never to go on the till.

The manager for most of her time there was Mr Matthews, who was fond of Phyl's cooking. Despite the fact that this small store had a cook to provide lunch, he would ask Phyl to cook Christmas Dinner for the staff. This she did with pride, taking in her own tins and utensils. Her Yorkshire Pudding (she was from Yorkshire) was, I think, the main reason she was asked to cook.

When the store closed it became an Iceland. Although the Worthing store was closer to home, I know Phyl preferred Goring and was sad to see it close: she worked there between 1962 and 1972, and at Worthing until retirement in 1981.'

Phyl Darlington (as told by her daughter)

Ooh – my head!

'I worked at the Penzance store (no. 651) from 1953 to 1986 and when I started in the stockroom there were four girls, two men and myself. I became the stockroom manager around 1970, but cutbacks over the years meant I was the only member of staff in the stockroom.

As I lived only a short distance from the store, I was the key holder and had to open the shop each morning at 8am to let the

Picture: Graham Rowe

Penzance shop staff at a social event in the Town Hall during the 1960s

Picture: Graham Rowe

Penzance shop staff helping residents of the Cheshire Home with their Christmas shopping during the 1960s

Ice lollies: a welcome break from the sales-floor at Penzance

staff in, and be the last to leave. On Saturdays I had to wear a suit and help out on the sales floor.

We had lovely Christmas parties for staff and families held at the Town Hall with nice dance bands and I always enjoyed the dancing and party spirit. All the staff looked forward to the parties: they were so much fun – until the next morning, when my head would ring when the girls rang the cash-till bells.'

Graham Rowe

Tears and laughter

'On the gift cards counter I was never allowed to be seen standing and not doing anything. We were always told to make ourselves busy, even if it meant cleaning the counter for the twentieth time. I would also help out, if I had no customers, on the sweet counter, which was next to me. This was in 1959 at the Cosham, Portsmouth, store, where I went to work when I was 17. My cousin Anita also worked there on the fruit counter. We have some funny memories from our days there. She fell down the stairs while getting fruit and blamed me for not saving her. Then when I fell over at the back of the shop, I thought I'd broken my ribs but she was in hysterics. I left Woolworth's because I used to be envious of all the young people my age on a Saturday coming into the shop enjoying themselves. I thought 'why am I working on a Saturday when I could be out enjoying myself too?"

Patricia White

Manager called me 'toots'

'My first manager at High Street, Erdington, Birmingham, was a man called Mr Barnes and he was the father-in-law of Charlie Drake, the TV star. Mr Barnes was a lovely man: he used to call my friend and I 'toots'. When I first started there, when I was 15, the top ten was played and my friend and I used to dance to the music behind the counters. I worked on the shop floor, then in the office and the freight office, eventually becoming a supervisor before I left when I was 21. On Mondays we had to do a checklist using a yellow booklet – we put a tick if we had the goods on sale and a cross if we didn't. Once a month we had to go to the stockroom and fill out binders, counting the stock and writing it in the binder. Every so often a superintendent used to visit the store. The checklist had to be correct; everything had to be on sale, including the entire colour range we stocked. I remember one superintendent asking us what we would do if there was a fire. I said I would run. He said 'I am being serious', and I said 'so am I'. If there was a fire, the staff had to take the money out of the tills and put it into little leather bags which were used when we cashed up each night. The supervisors then had to collect the bags. Working at Woolworth's was great fun – but on Saturdays the store was so full of customers you couldn't get off the counter to go to lunch.'

Gail Ashton

Still in touch

'My mother Mary Grist worked at the Amersham branch of Woolworth's from 1972 until she retired in September 1986. She thoroughly enjoyed her time there. Her managers were Messrs Sweeting, Bullock, Pughe, Maudsley, Cleveland and Maller. She has particularly fond memories of Mr Bullock and is still in touch with several of the girls she used to work with: most of them are over 80 now and a couple are well into their 90s. I was a Saturday girl with my friend Helen, and I worked there from 1967 to 1969.'

Vivien H

Good deeds

'In December 1968, members of staff at the Camarthen branch volunteered to chaperone residents of Combe Cheshire Home for the aged to do some Christmas shopping during closing hours. Thursday was half-day in Carmarthen. The mayor and mayoress came, and two police constables. I was only 15 years old at the time. It was a lovely time working in this store along with my sister.'

Sheila Evans

Picture: Sheila Evans

Sheila Evans, aged 15

Picture: Sheila Evans

Carmarthen staff in 1968, helping customers from the Combe Cheshire Home for the aged to do some Christmas shopping. The mayor and mayoress turned out for the occasion, as did PC Ronw James. The store manager, Mr Rickets, can be seen standing on the far left

Overtime was part of the job

'Woolworth's policy was for their future managers to start on the shop floor as a stockroom assistant: if a young man or woman showed promise, they would be promoted. I started as a Saturday boy at Redhill in July 1950, then went full-time once I'd left school. Eventually I became store manager, first at Banstead (no. 737) and then at North Cheam (no. 687).

The manager at Redhill, Mr Robert Gibbons, was a very stern serious man who demanded high standards from his staff. I clearly remember him saying to me that when I made a mistake it was a learning process, and I was not to make the same mistake again. In those days our store opening hours were 9am – 5.30pm daily and 9am – 1pm on Wednesdays. We had to be off the premises by 2pm at the latest as, even in those days, I believe we would be breaking the Shop Act if we were there after that time. With my stockroom manager, Mr Arthur Warwick (his wife Hilda was chief cashier), I worked many hours longer than we were paid for, as I had to make sure the sales floor had been swept and cleared of rubbish ready for the next day's trading, before I could go home.

One of my many early duties was to help Mr Warwick unload the many delivery vehicles that would pull up outside the lift door, which opened directly on to the street. This involved moving many different-sized packages, which varied greatly in weight. We didn't have any modern equipment like pallet trucks, only one medium-sized sack truck. British Rail goods lorries delivered most of our stock from the local rail depot. At times the packages arrived in very poor condition, either soaked with rainwater or having been torn open by railway employees seeking something of value. More valuable items were usually sent by passenger train. We also had direct deliveries and weekly van-sales from many suppliers including Cadbury's, Rowntrees, Brooke Bond, J Lyons, Woodgrange Tinware, and Ever Ready Batteries. One other delivery that was always a major problem was a full container from Welsh Tinplate of enamelware. This had to be booked in at a time when all the stockroom staff were available to unload it, as it was all loose inside the container, packed in huge amounts of straw to try and prevent the items being damaged. There were always several pieces chipped which the store had to try and claim for, mostly unsuccessfully.

When biscuits were delivered from Hughes & Sons in Birmingham, huge queues would form in the shop, as biscuits were still on ration. These were packed loose in silver-lined boxes and had to be weighed to the customer's requirements. Some customers would wait or come back the next day and ask if there were any broken biscuits, which were sold at half price. The store manager didn't like this being done as no allowance was made for this loss, and he instructed the staff to mix a few broken ones with the whole ones, thus keeping sales of broken ones to a minimum.

Several times a week I escorted the manager to the bank, which was a fair walk. I had to bring back the large amounts of copper and silver coins that the store required, usually carrying one large cotton bag on each shoulder.

One summer we had a serious infestation of cockroaches on the sales floor; they came from underneath the ice-cream refrigerator which was next to the confectionery counter. The store cleaner and I would attempt to sweep them up and dispose of them before they escaped under the wooden floor boards again. They were treated with powder sprays but it took some years before they were no longer a problem. It was believed that the store had been built on an old bakery, and they only managed to come up through the floor as the wooden floor deteriorated.

One of the worst jobs my stockroom manager and I had to do every six weeks or so, after we closed on a Saturday and all the shop floor assistants had left, was to spray special oil on to the wooden sales floor area, to try to prevent it drying out too much. It helped to reduce the amount of dust that went up in the air when I swept the floor daily. On Monday mornings before the store opened, I would have to spread felspar (a grit-like substance) liberally on the floor to stop any customers or staff slipping over. At the end of the day I had to sweep it all up again – what a job!

In the winter the sales floor was heated by gas lamps hanging from the ceiling, and in the early days I had to re-light the pilot lights every morning, as the gas and electricity was turned off every night. Eventually the utilities were left on, so I only had to get a hook and pull the chains down in the morning. They were also used as emergency lighting in case we had any power cuts, as we did sometimes in those days. Some years later, floor gas heaters were installed in the sales area. During a heavy rain-storm the internal drains were blocked (due to a cleaner emptying her bucket of water out and the dirty cloths as well) and the rain came through onto the sales floor and nearly filled some of the gas light-globes up. A terrible mess to clear up.

There was no heating in the stockrooms which were immediately under a flat roof, so in the winter with snow or heavy frosts on the roof, it used to get very cold, and the stockroom staff were allowed to wear hats, coats and mittens or gloves to try and keep warm. We were allowed extra Oxo breaks at these times, which the store paid for. Eventually we were allowed two gas fires, which did help to keep the stockroom warmer.

Very occasionally I was instructed by the manager to deliver special orders. I did this on a bicycle, just like Granville's in *Open all Hours* although I never met an attractive young lady. One day I went out and couldn't find the address: I got absolutely soaked in the rain on the way back, only to find the details had been incorrectly written on the delivery note.

One summer evening the manager wanted to get away

promptly after the 5.30pm closure so he could go to an area meeting. Unfortunately one of the sales staff, who was trying to finish her stock and order folders before she went on holiday, wasn't told, and she was locked in the upstairs stockroom. She raised the alarm by opening one of the windows on the High Street side and attracting the attention of a member of the public below. The police managed to contact another key-holder who arrived, much to everyone's relief, after about an hour.

Stocktaking was also an arduous task which was done immediately after Christmas. We only had Christmas Day and Boxing Day off – even if the 27th was a Sunday we had to start the stocktaking as it had to be finished by the 31st and the inventory book taken up to Head Office. A lot of preparation work had to be done in the stockroom with all the various departments lined up and ticketed with an inventory label which had to be completed with all the details of the item, including the cost price which was written in an alphabetical code that only a few senior staff knew. When the department had been counted and double-checked, it was ready for the manager or assistant manager to call out to an office girl who would be sitting at a table in the aisle of that particular department in the stockroom. She recorded the details of each item –a long and laborious task. In later years this was much improved, as the manager or his assistant would tear off the slips after checking the details, then take them to an office area where members of staff sitting in comfort would record them.

When the department had been completed, the inventory stock-sheets would be taken to a quiet area where a comptometer operator would extend them at selling price and total all the sheets up for each department. The counters were done in a similar way, only recording the selling price and quantity of the item. The inventory book would then have been made up with the various purchases, debits and sales figures to give the stock result, which normally was between one and one-and-a-half percent of the total store sales. In later years for various reasons which were not totally honest, many stores would bring in much improved results, sometimes even 'overages' were recorded. These were the clever managers who were generally promoted to higher office.

In May 1953, just before I was due to start my National Service, I was sent to store no. 682 at Epsom to help staff sort out the stockroom, which was on the top two of the five-storey building. The two lower ones were sales floors and the middle one contained offices and staff areas. This was a real challenge for me, as the stockroom was very untidy, with many deliveries waiting to be unpacked and checked against the invoice, before being passed for payment. There were also huge quantities of returnable empties that needed packing up and labelling to be returned to their respective suppliers. There was one very unpleasant incident which still comes to mind, in the early days of my work there, I had a very large goods delivery, and several lifts full of packages to take up and unload. There were two large bags of potting compost which weighed 1.5 hundredweight each and were too awkward to get on the lift. To save the lorry driver waiting any longer, as he had several more deliveries to make, I left them outside in an alcove, to collect after I had emptied the lift. When I came back some 20 minutes later they had gone. Even at that young age I knew somebody couldn't have stolen them, so I went into the store looking for them. To my delight they had been moved downstairs into the assistant manager's office. Imagine his surprise when he questioned me later regarding the missing bags, and I pointed them out to him in the correct place in the stockroom. This incident, I understand, was reported to the area superintendent, who reprimanded him for his actions.

After my two years' National Service I restarted at Redhill and worked in various departments on the sales floor, my job being mainly to ensure that fast-selling lines were constantly refilled. Christmas was such a busy time that it was virtually impossible to get from the stairs and lift from the stockroom to the sales counters, because of all the customers. We had no internal communication between the sales floor and stockroom in those days, except for the phone line in the cash office, but staff were not allowed into the room when cash was being counted. Many times I had to shout up the lift shaft to the stockroom and hope somebody would hear me as it was too far to keep running up and down stairs.

I started dating a young, slim girl from the invoice office: her name was Mary and she had a beautiful smile. Mary had been a Saturday girl when the head cashier had suggested that, as Mary hadn't a full-time job to go to, she might like to stay on. She was pleased to accept – and what a marvellous decision that was. Mary has been my lovely wife for 50 years now. A few months after I first asked Mary out, I was promoted to store no. 64 at Tooting Broadway as a trainee manager under the strong guidance of a Mr W Woolway. The journey from Salfords in Surrey involved three train changes and a short underground journey. I really enjoyed working in the busy store, spending time on all the various departments, learning the display and layout techniques and the rate of sale of fast-selling lines. There was a great team of staff working together to make a success of the store, not only for the excellent manager but for everyone's job satisfaction.

What a challenge it was in those days to try and order the correct mix of the new lines that were arriving regularly, all done by counting and checking regularly each individual item's rate of sale – there were no computers in those days to do 'stock and order' for you. The popular plain and floral colours in the various styles of plastic lampshades were selling really well. The new polythene ranges of kitchenware came in, and out went the old enamelware buckets and bowls With the start of the DIY explosion, new colours were available in a huge paint range. And, of course, the new soap-powder ranges that would wash clothes 'whiter than white'. We also stocked a marvellous range of colours and designs in the new self-adhesive Contact shelf and table-covering range, where we had a full-time assistant employed just to serve this product.

The hardware department, Dept 28, was a real challenge to try and keep the huge range of items in stock, particularly all the screws from Guest Keen and Nettllefold, who wanted four weeks or more from the date of our order to delivery, and the brass curtain-rail range and accessories from Harrison and Sons of Birmingham, who took even longer sometimes.

I trained on the other departments and found them all really interesting and challenging in their own way: haberdashery, for example, with all the new ranges of fish-eye polyester buttons, new colours of knitting wool, and improved ranges of zips. What a marvellous department, even for a young man to be involved in. It did have its problems though, as all members of staff, even stockroom staff, were expected to get on the island counters and serve when the regular staff were unable to cope. At one of these times the 'haby' counter was really busy: being a young lad I was sent down to the opposite end to where the STs were displayed. You can imagine my embarrassment when the first customer I went to serve, who was a rather large Jamaican lady, called out in a loud voice, 'two packs of size two Dr White's please'.

The footwear ranges were largely imported from one of Woolworth's specially registered import companies, and the plimsolls and Wellingtons largely came from the Far East. These were usually prepacked in three different assorted size cases, and the store had to work out the best cases to order to balance up their existing stocks. Due to shipping difficulties, delivery was often four or five months after ordering. A heavy fall of snow would have customers buying up stocks of Wellingtons we'd had in the stockroom for over two years, and we often sold out before we could get replacement supplies.

One of the new and popular ranges when we started selling more grocery items were Birds Eye frozen foods. Another was a trial line of tuna fish; we had one case of 48 tins and sold out in less than a day. The manager decided this was going to be a real winner and ordered 40 cases. When the delivery arrived, an eight-foot end display was cleared and piled high with tins of tuna fish. Our sales were fantastic and brought a head office sales sheet shortly afterwards in the post, praising the wonderful sales figure. Sometimes these sales sheets, based on reports from the store, weren't always true, and were just a way of getting the store in the headlines.

We had a superb range of Easter Eggs, not just from Cadbury's, Frys, Mackintosh and Rowntrees, as these were in short supply, but also we had our Woolworth's own brand range made by the Shuttleworth Confectionery Company. Huge quantities were sold especially in the last week before Easter and stocks had to be counted and checked regularly against last year's sales to ensure we had sufficient to maximise sales, and – if not – attempt to obtain more supplies from other stores who were overstocked.

Superintendents were responsible for several stores that varied in size from those classed as 'super stores' down to the small 'class 5' stores. Their job was to visit regularly to ensure the stores were kept up to a good standard and well managed. They would arrive generally unannounced, though sometimes managers got a tip-off that a visit was imminent. They used a 'spot list', generally a seasonal list covering every department, and a 'checking list', which covered a large basic range of items and colours and sizes. As soon as staff knew about this they would busily check their department lists to see what they were short of and attempt to obtain supplies from other local Woolworth's stores. I am sure they knew what went on, as they would have done the same when they were managers. Sometimes quantities were so small that the department head would wait till the superintendent had started his check, before putting them out on display, in case they were sold before he came to check that particular item.

Most of these men 'on the road', as it was termed, would be most helpful in helping the store get higher standards, and would give an honest report on the store's general operation, without being too nitpicky, Mr D Brown, Mr A J Ray and Mr R Bell were in this category, although if there was something really amiss, then you had to look out! Some others were only interested in their own career and wanted to show how good they were at pointing out every fault they could find, rather than come to the aid of a manager in difficulties.

From time to time the assistant managers went out to the smaller stores so that small store managers could have their holidays. One of my many memorable pro-tem management relief duties was in March 1958 when, despite Mr Woolway having staff shortages, he agreed that I could help out Mr Barter at Surbiton. Mr Barter was so impressed with my efforts – a sales increase of more than 10 percent for the week putting the store in the black for the first time – that he wrote a letter of thanks.

There was a terrible accident one day in the store: a service engineer came to repair one of the two large soft-mix ice-cream machines, which stood on a raised platform about a foot high. The engineer took the cover off the back and side of the motor, and started it up. Unfortunately as he turned on the raised platform, his foot slipped and his hand was trapped in the belting around the drive wheels. There was a terrible mess with blood everywhere, and staff rushed to his aid to stem the flow with linen towels. An ambulance arrived quickly and he was taken to the local Accident and Emergency at great speed. It was later reported that he had lost two fingers completely.

After further training and experience I was promoted to assistant manager at Wimbledon under Mr Piet, another experienced manager, who again was most helpful and gave me plenty of opportunities to broaden my experience and knowledge. In a relatively short time I became deputy manager at Kingston on Thames. This was a 'super super' store, under Mr Tom Hockham, a very senior manager of some note. He had built up an excellent staff, who virtually ran the store for him. Sales were good and my knowledge and experience continued to improve. Mr Hockman had a favourite saying whenever he was unimpressed with a staff member's attempt to do something: 'That's about as much good as nothing', he'd say.

Wimbledon had fixtures and fittings that were in urgent need of replacing. This involved much weekend work and overtime, so as not to inconvenience the customers too much when replacing the counters and with putting down modern stone tiling in place of the old wooden flooring. When it was all finished, the store looked magnificent. The customers flooded in and sales improved dramatically. When Mr Hockham retired, he was replaced by Mr Bill Gwynne, a delightful Welshman, who had been a store manager since 1935. He was very reluctant to take over the store, not because he wasn't capable but because he only had three or four years or so before he also retired, and he felt the store needed a younger man with energy and enthusiasm. He came from the Hammersmith store and it had taken him three years to get the staff conforming to his excellent work practices. I worked really well with him and respected him greatly: he had different ideas from Mr Hockham and the staff took to them enthusiastically. One of his regular sayings was 'if the current task isn't necessary then don't do it: find a more important one to do'.

One weekend we had a break-in. When we returned to work on the Monday we saw ladders, huge gas bottles and cables stretching up to a window high above ground level, which was the invoice office. The intruders had travelled by boat up the Thames which ran at the back of the store. They had blacked out the windows with thick black paint and cut open one safe. Unfortunately for them, the safe they opened only contained the ledgers; they had tried the other safe, but not succeeded.

Shortly after Mr Gwynne took over, I decided to purchase my first car, a sit-up-and-beg Ford Popular, but I needed to borrow £200 from the Midland Bank. I was really disappointed when they refused, as I had opened the account shortly after finishing my National Service, and paid money in regularly. I mentioned this to Mr Gwynne and he immediately phoned the local National Westminster Bank manager where we banked and explained my situation to him: he asked for me to go round immediately. I arrived promptly and was shown into his office. He gave me an application form to fill in and the money was in my account by the morning. Once I bought the car I would sometimes pick up Mr Gwynne from his home on way in from Salfords, as my normal route went past his house.

Just after Christmas 1962, on the Sunday we were due to start stocktaking, it started snowing about 6.30am and when I tried to climb Reigate Hill I only got halfway up. There were very few gritting lorries in those days, and if one was gritting it was done by two men shovelling rock salt out of the back of a lorry. I turned back round to find another route via Leatherhead, as the roads were much flatter and hopefully passable. I got to the store at about 8.45am to cheers from the staff, as at that time I was one of the only two key-holders.

All the staff who were due to work on that Sunday arrived to start the stocktaking, but more snow fell during the day and we heard that the buses were going to stop running at 5.30pm due to

Picture: Alan Munn

Christmas Party time at the Lakers Hotel for Redhill workers. A youthful Alan Munn can be seen standing top right. The store manager, Mr R S Gibbons – clearly too dignified to wear his party hat – is seated in the front row on the left

the terrible road conditions. Staff went home early, but Mr Gwynne and I decided to stay the night in the store, as we would have never have arrived on time in the morning. We locked all the doors, had something to eat, did some more work till late and slept in the upstairs sick-room: it had only one small heater, a couch and a wooden arm chair. Guess who had the couch? I slept very badly as he was snoring and the gale-force wind was making all sorts of noises and bangs, apart from the normal cooling-down sounds of a building at night. But the snow cleared, we returned home safely the following day, and the stocktaking was completed on time.

In 1963 I was promoted to manager of store no. 737 at Banstead, a fairly small store, but one with plenty of opportunities for a new manager to 'have a go' with some of the new ranges. For instance, we started selling a restricted range of fruit and vegetables, which proved very popular with our customers, especially when I found a local smallholder was interested in selling his summer salad items direct to us. Some special-offer grocery lines were also now available which brought more customers in, which meant they purchased other higher-profit lines as well. Toiletries were also being made available at competitive prices, which increased our customers' interest. I finished the year with a sales increase of over 16 percent and, more importantly, with net profits up by 29 percent.

Another promotion followed, this time to a much busier store at North Cheam, but there was a lot of unease already beginning to creep in amongst the local managers. Woolworth's managers had always been very well paid, but senior head management did not continue that policy, and new managers worked for a lot less than their predecessors – even bonuses were cut. Sales increases were harder to come by too, as competition from other retailers was hotting up and we were being undercut on popular ranges. New companies were on the scene and advertising for experienced managers and staff –one of these was a grocery company called Elmo, based in the Norfolk-Suffolk area. They were offering good money and prospects to join their growing operation, so I gave in my notice and left the company I had loved working for, I was amazed, having worked for Woolworth's for 15 years, that nobody contacted me to talk things over, or to find out why. All I received was a standard letter from the district manager accepting my resignation and wishing me well. Other managers phoned me up to say they admired my decision, and would seriously consider their position, as they didn't fancy spending the next 30 years with FWW the way things were going.

Where did it all go wrong, in my own humble opinion? The executive office many years ago should have employed a top marketing director from outside the company to advise on a viable future: as it was, the company management continued doing what they thought was best, based on their own Woolworth's experience. I probably would have done the same. We owned most of our store sites and had prime positions in many large towns. Over the years we sold them and then paid rent instead, surely not a good move. We had to challenge the new companies and not pull out of selling groceries and other lower-profit food ranges: after all everyone has to eat. Look at these retail giants of today Tesco and Asda, which started as little corner shops selling volume quantities of lower-profit items which brought customers into their shops. Woolworth's seemed only to be interested in selling high-profit goods. As a former store manager, I have watched Woolie's gradually and sadly keep changing their marketing polices and ranges, with very little success and now finally – through bad management and leadership from the top – they have finally closed.'

Alan Munn

Up on the roof

'In the summer at Woolworth's in Minehead, we used to take our lunch breaks out on the flat roof. I worked there from 1959, when I started as a stockroom junior, until 1962 when I ended up as stockroom manageress.'

Pamela Griffiths

Picture: Ken Roberts

Two pals dressed in the new Woolworth's uniforms: Freda Roberts and Miss E Fisher relax in the back yard of the Sherborne store in 1940

Our little oasis

'In 1938, the year that F W Woolworth's was being built in Cheap Street in Sherborne, Dorset, I applied to become a counter assistant, working my way up to become a supervisor. The back yard of the store was an oasis of relaxation for members of staff to relax and chat together in between busy hours spent behind the counter. The war meant that I had to transfer to the local factory of Westland, making Spitfire fighter planes, but in 1955 I was asked if I would like to go back and work for Woolworth's. I started back as a part-time sales assistant, then went full-time and became staff supervisor, a job I retained until retirement in March 1981.'

The late Freda Roberts,
paraphrased from notes in her photo-
graph album kindly lent by her son

Picture: Ken Roberts

Sophie Wilding, Freda Roberts, Maria Brittain and Gertie Fisher at the rear of the Sherborne store, on 26 March 1940

Picture: Ken Roberts

Sherborne shop staff in their new premises in Cheap Street in 1966. Freda Roberts is seated third from left in the second row, next to the manager Mr B J Skeet

All because the gentleman loved Milk Tray

'My main responsibility at the Woolworth's store on Wembley High Road was to crush all the cardboard boxes and packaging which the store accumulated each day, using an industrial crusher in the basement. I recall being submerged by it all each morning. By the late afternoon I was just beginning to make an impression. The machine had a safety gate and automatically secured the bales of packaging before I opened the gate and pushed the bales out. It was hot and unpleasant work, but I knew no different at the time.

One morning on my way to the basement, I passed by a trolley full of confectionery and couldn't resist taking a box of Cadbury's Milk Tray with me down to the basement. I then spent the rest of the morning pigging out on my ill-gotten gains. The theft was noted, but I was quite certain I would not be found out, as long as I disposed of the empty box into the crusher.

Picture: Lorna Robson

Lorna Robson (far right on top row) at the Crook branch in the 1960s. The team are assembled with Mr O'Leary, the manager, to celebrate 21 years of service by office staff-member Marjorie Best (second from right in the bottom row)

The manager asked me to assist him each Friday in carrying the week's takings to the bank situated a few hundred yards along the High Street. The cash was placed in a leather case, which was then secured with a line to my wrist. If the line became detached, a piercing alarm would sound. I thought at the time that it was quite exciting, but with hindsight it was a very risky operation. I stayed at Woolworth's for three months – this was in 1965 between leaving school and going on to college.'

Ian Grierson

A Saturday girl for every counter

'At the Crook branch, where I worked from about 1961–68, we had all separate counters with an assistant for each one, including a Saturday girl. Ours was just a small store but we had great times there. Our Saturday girls were Jean Holiday, Lorraine Singlewood, Margaret Gray, Brenda Taylor and Kathleen Payne. I left in 1968 and I believe the store closed in the 1970s.'

Lorna Robson

Romance on the biscuit counter

'I met a lot of nice people at Woolworth's in Middlesbrough, including the man who was to become my husband. I worked there for 12 years from 1966 to 1978, starting on the biscuit counter and finishing by becoming a supervisor in the same department. My mother, sister and two sister-in-laws also worked in the same store.'

Elaine Scott

I'll just call you Fred

'The sweets counter was my favourite: that's where I developed my sweet tooth from all the sampling. I remember Mint Imperials and Bonbons: they were sold for 2d a quarter and you had to go upstairs to weigh them before putting them into little bags. I had started out in 1940 on the hardware counter, cutting keys. There was a supervisor called Winnie Telford, and because she decided it would be too confusing to have two 'Winnies' in the store, so she said she would call me Fred instead. They were happy times – we use to sit on the big window sills watching life go by on busy Clayton Street. My only sad memory was when my uniform skirt was stolen one Christmas.'

Winifred Mullen

Belfast staff outside the County Down station during the late 1930s or early 1940s

Adella Black and her colleagues at a staff party at the Belfast store

Walking the floor

'My great aunt Adella Black, who was born 1894 in the Townland of Corkhill, Kildress, worked as a 'floor-walker' in the Belfast store – today she would have been called a supervisor. She was there most of her working life. Her home was in Cookstown, County Tyrone.'

Dorothy Fleming

Some hair cream please – and will you marry me?

'I started work in the Frome branch of Woolworth's in 1936 at the age of 16 and it is where I met my husband to whom I have been married to for 68 years. I was on the toiletry counter and he used to come in on Saturdays for his razor blades and hair cream. I worked there until 1941 when I had to register for war work, and joined the ATS. I did Fire Watching on the roof of the Frome store.'

Edna Prescott

The 39 Tills

'At the old Taunton branch in East Street, I worked in the office for a couple of years, from 1959 to 1961. I remember that in those days, the store had 39 tills.'

Jill Hutchings

Picture: Jill Hutchings

A party at the County Hotel for staff of the East Street, Taunton, branch in 1959

Mind the mice

'Whitby was a holiday and fishing town, and advertising a 'summer job' was a way of getting rid of unwanted staff in September. However, I felt I was lucky to get the job: I was 15 in 1955 and my wages at Woolies were £2 1s 9d, I kept 11s 9d and my mum had £1 10 shillings – known as thirty bob. We wore red overalls, which we had to ask permission to take home to wash.

All the staff were women except for the manager and the stock-boy, a handsome lad of good family and public school education, and we lasses all had our eyes on him. We wrote a stock list every day and the stock boy brought it the next day. I started work on the toiletries counter upstairs and then moved downstairs to the sweets. We had mice under the sweets counter and if I dropped any money I was frightened to kneel down and look for it.

We had to be precise with our weighing, as most of our sweets were loose, and had to cut some sweets in half so the quarter-pound would not be overweight. An irate customer reported me to the manager because she thought it was stupid.

Whitby Woolies was on two floors and if the manager leaned over the stairs, he could see behind every counter because of the mirrors around the store. I was lucky to be interviewed by an area manager about full time work, I told her I thought Woolies was wonderful and I got a permanent job.

We did stock-taking on New Year's Eve and we all had to work until it was done: most of the girls came ready dressed for the New Year's dance, and we all hoped to be done in time for a quick bop and a kiss.

The shop floor was dark brown wood and we took turns to sweep it at the end of the day. The stock-boy oiled it once a month and we girls had to scrub a four-inch strip of floor around our counters. Woe betide anyone who did six inches like me.

Sometimes I had to go to the stock room for supplies. The stairs leading up to it were narrow, and stock was put into a heavy wicker basket on wheels with a rope handle. Complete with basket, I would get the lift down to the ground floor, but often could not get the door open. After shouting and banging and not being heard, I would take the lift back up and try the stairs with the stock basket dangling in front, it being heavier than me. Sometimes I fell down with it, or sometimes I'd be lucky and someone would help me, and then I would be told off for being away too long.

I worked on the ice-cream counter and the haberdashery, I had to know the price and place of each item, and we also had diagrams to follow for where everything had to be. When we had a sale, most of the goods were especially brought in and we were not allowed to buy anything, so our family had to join the queue outside and push like the rest.

Before they introduced clocking-in, we had to write our names in a book for 'in' and 'out'. One of the girls got locked in the store – nobody checked or shouted upstairs and the boss assumed everyone had gone home and locked up. She banged on the glass doors but no-one saw or heard her. She was a bit frightened that she would see the much-talked-about ghost, so she used the telephone in the open office and phoned for help.'

Margaret Davies

You had to eat, sleep and drink Woolworths

'My first job, at 14 years of age, was at Vickers Armstrong Supermarine making Spitfire aircraft. This was during the war. I did my National Service in the Royal Navy, but when I returned to civilian life, there was no longer a job in the aircraft industry. This led me to answer an advertisement for a post as stockroom manager at the Southampton branch of Woolworth's. In due course I attended an interview with Mr Brown, the manager at the Above Bargate store (no. 124). There were two of us at the interview – myself and Fred Bishop – and we were both taken on 'on probation'. Woolworth's unwritten policy was to overload their prospective management staff so that those not prepared to eat, sleep and drink Woolworth's would soon leave. As it happened, Fred Bishop played trumpet in a dance band and found that when the shop closed at 5pm you were expected to work on without overtime. This interfered with his band commitments and he quickly resigned.

The Above Bargate store was a hastily built, single storey

concrete block, a long narrow 'shed' in the middle of a bomb-site with no other buildings around. It was constructed over the cellars of the original pre-war building. The labyrinth of cellars was below ground, dimly lit, with no windows, and fitted out with alleyways and shelves to make a stockroom. Access to the stockroom from the street was down a slope at the rear of the building with a single flight of stairs going up into the shop.

All deliveries in those days were by British Railways lorry, the goods being manhandled down the slope and into the unpacking space. The stockroom staff consisted of myself, under the misnomer of manager (really a working factotum) plus two store boys and three girls. My day started at 7am when I left home to cycle the six miles to Southampton in order to start work at 8am. The first task on arrival was to remove the fire buckets, then to fill the tea-bar boiler with water, open the tea-bar kitchen, and bring in the kitchen supplies which would have been left outside by the tradesmen and baker.

In those days biscuits were supplied loose in cardboard cartons, so any cardboard had to be sorted out and placed in the hand-operated press, bound with thin wire and stowed on one side of the bay to await collection. The first rush was when the counter girls arrived and found they had not ordered enough items the previous day to fill the counter. By that time, deliveries were arriving and the lorry had to be unloaded quickly to stop the road becoming blocked.

When wire crates of crockery and kitchenware were delivered, the crates had to be eased off the lorry by hand with no equipment, onto slides and down the slope to be unpacked. On the same lorry would be loads of small packages that had to be counted and receipts given to the driver. We could then start opening the packages. Individual items of crockery and kitchenware were packed in straw, so the stockroom soon began to look like a farmyard. The contents of each package was checked against the supplier's invoice and discrepancy reports raised to cover shortages or damage. The items themselves were loaded into wicker baskets which ran on four castors, and removed to the correct storage area. Then one sample from each delivery was sent up to the departmental supervisor to indicate that a new delivery had been received. The arrival of scarce items such as crockery or enamel kitchenware was quite an event, which required a whole counter to be cleared to make the necessary space. The demand was so great that the stockroom staff were hard-pressed to keep the counter supplied.

As the day progressed, counter girls would come down to the stockroom to replenish their stock. This was much frowned on by the supervisor, as it reduced the staff available to serve on the counter. Late in the afternoon the girls would again come down, one by one, to select and load into the wicker baskets stock required for the following day. Which in due course the stockroom staff had to manhandle up the stairs for delivery to the appropriate counter.

At closing time there would be a scramble to fill the counters ready for the following day and send the empty baskets back to the stockroom. Once the shop was shut, every counter was covered with a dustsheet and the stockroom staff could sweep the floor, place out the fire buckets and prepare the shop and stockroom for the following day.

During the summer months of the early 1950s the local fishmonger delivered to the stockroom big cubes of ice wrapped in sacking. The ice was split up with an pick and the pieces put into a dustbin with bottles of soft drinks. The bin was placed on the pavement outside the front of the shop. At the same time, an ice-cream cabinet was hauled down the front steps on two planks of wood, where an assistant was allocated to sell the drinks and ice cream. This of course presented stockroom staff with an all-day task keeping the supplies topped up.

The manager felt that ladies were embarrassed when buying sanitary towels from the counter, so he decided that just one of each type should be on display: the main stock, already wrapped, would be served discreetly from under the counter. This was very popular with the customers and improved sales.

Another recognised ploy for items which were overstocked, or needed to be sold quickly, was not to lay them out neatly but to pile them up on an end-of-counter display where customers could pick them up and handle them before purchase. This proved to be a very successful method of moving stock.

The present method of selling is for each item to be individually priced and for the customer to pay at a central point. In the 1950s purchases were paid for direct to the shop assistant at the counter, so the items did not need a price ticket attached. The goods were neatly laid out in separate sections according to range, type and size. The price of any group of items was shown on a price ticket slotted into a metal stand placed at the back of the display. The counters were laid out throughout the store as separate islands, with two long sides and two shorter ends. This left a central space on each island from where the assistant served the customers and took the money. Each assistant had her own till. The surface of each counter was covered with moveable counter blocks, so that glass dividing pieces could be slotted in, creating sub-sections in which to display the goods. This system made it very easy to increase or decrease the individual display area because to re-lay a full counter was a major operation.

Wednesday was early closing, so this gave the manager the opportunity to detail stockroom staff to clean the concrete tea-bar kitchen floor with a solution of caustic soda and water. This removed the grease from the floor and also the stitching from the crêpe soled shoes, which were then in fashion, so in due course the soles fell off. The so-called half-day soon became a full working day without overtime. When I arrived home about 4pm on my half day, my mother always asked why I was so 'early' and whether I had been given the sack.

Stock control was exercised by the departmental supervisor with a checklist system. The list was a yellow cardboard sheet divided into squares, the left-hand column showing items people expected to find in a Woolworth's store, plus additional items appropriate to the size of the store and its location. For example a seaside store would hold a different range of additional items from an inland store. It was the departmental supervisor's job to see that all the items on the list were on display, then to count the stockroom and fill in the appropriate square on the checklist. As the stock became low this was entered on the checklist and an order placed in the file of the company contracted to supply the goods. Some items, such as Christmas and Easter cards, and springtime seeds, were recorded separately to make it easier to identify the best-sellers when re-ordering for the following year.

During the early 1950s Woolworth's were opening new stores in quick succession. This meant that existing staff were deployed to prepare the new stores for opening. By that time I had obtained a motorcycle, so I was called on to set up the stockrooms in the new stores at Winchester, Lymington and Woolston and also assist the new stockroom manager in the Above Bargate store. After that flurry of activity, I was promoted to the post of shop walker at Above Bargate and was required to wear a white shirt, collar and tie, and the only suit I possessed. The crêpe-soled shoes had to go, being replaced by polished black leather.

I received an increase in pay but no decrease in hours. At that time a salary of £8 per week was good but, when divided by the hours worked, it was not very rewarding.

In my new position I assisted the deputy manager on the shop floor and became the supervisor for a number of counters. This brought me into closer contact with the shop staff, who were easily identifiable by their maroon uniforms. The cash-office staff and departmental supervisors wore blue overalls. Those serving on the cosmetics counter, biscuits, sweets, and tea-bar wore white. All overalls were without pockets for obvious reasons. At certain periods during the day I had to escort the cash-office clerk when removing the money and the till-roll from the cash registers. The till rolls recorded every transaction rung up through the till. As each department counter had its own till it was easy to identify discrepancies between the money taken and the total shown on the till roll. If this pointed to a repeated series of errors, the manager would dismiss the assistant without explanation. The cash remained in the safe overnight and the following morning I would either walk or take a bus to the bank with the money locked in a Gladstone bag secured to my waist by a chain.

At Christmas or when Southampton Football Club were playing at home, Woolworth's became so crowded that the manager introduced a one-way system, ushering the shoppers through the entrance to shuffle down one side of this long narrow building, and along the bottom past the tea-bar where customers were standing drinking their tea with their cups and plates resting on a narrow shelf fixed to the wall. They would then be pressed up the far side and out through the front door. A certain amount of unofficial 'price crowding' took place, where a penny or so was added to the authorised selling price. This happened particularly on birthday cards and garden seeds where it was not so obvious. When the district manager paid a visit, there was a scramble to get the prices changed back to the correct amount.

In the early 1950s the bomb damaged commercial areas of Southampton were rebuilt and part of the scheme was for a new Woolworth's, built on a site adjacent to and incorporating the old store. The disruption was immense: counters had to be moved, lighting adjusted and parts of walls taken down. Everything got covered in dust. Things began to change: our old manager retired, and a 'new broom' arrived. A gleaming new shop opened next door, putting our 'shed' to shame. Customers now had a choice of where to shop and takings went down. With the new manager pushing to maintain the business, the atmosphere became very strained. I eventually got fed up with it and one day went to lunch and never returned. They still owe me a week's pay. One week after leaving, I received a letter from my old manager, inviting me for tea and to discuss my future. He said he thought I was a little hasty and he had taken the liberty of writing to Head Office asking them to review my resignation.

A letter arrived from the company offering me the position of stockroom manager in the Oxford Street store in London. I gave this some thought but concluded it could be a downward step, requiring me to march back up the hierarchy to reach the same position as when I left. Instead, I joined the Royal Fleet Auxiliary: this took me to Christmas Island in the Pacific for the last UK Atomic bomb test. I subsequently saw service in Bahrain, Aden, Mombassa, Mauritius and a period of secondment to the Libyan Navy, as well as serving in all of the Dockyards at home. Looking back, I think I made a fair swap.'

Harold Gilham

Leave my lampshades alone!

'My friend Annie and I came down from Scotland in 1982 and worked over the festive season in the Southsea branch of Woolworth's. I worked on the lampshades and electrical aisles, and woe betide anyone who messed up my lampshades. It gave us the start to our new lives in the south. We have fond and fun memories working there, also some fuzzy memories too – being in our 20s, we did party hard. We went our separate ways for years, but now meet up regularly for a good old reminiscising session. We remember someone called Lyn who had worked there for years and others (known as The Blondes), though we have long forgotten their names'.

Susan Hill and Anne Hunt

No more biscuits for me

'I worked on loose biscuits and cakes in the London Road, Portsmouth, store and had to wear a horrible yellow overall and hat. I never touched biscuits for years afterwards'.

Rita Waight

One boy and 35 girls

'I was 15 in 1944 when I started work as a stockroom boy at Woolworth's in Scunthorpe. It was my second real job after leaving school prematurely, aged 13. My first had been as a farm labourer in Norfolk. At Woolworth's I very soon realised that I was the only boy among 35 girls – what a job! The first day I was completely whacked out after working indoors for the first time in years. Nothing to do with the girls, I hasten to say. At one time, half the family seemed to be working there. There was myself, my sister Daphne, cousin Leona and her mother, and my Aunt Vera (the cook). Also my mother spent a lot of time there in the lunch hours, reading the fortunes of the girls and manageress in the 'tea leaves', much to my embarrassment.

On my very first day, one of the girls, Sandy Sanderson, greeted me: 'I know you! You're one of the little buggers who nicks foreign stamps off my counter'! She didn't tell the manageress thank goodness, so I didn't lose my job on the first day.

My main duties as the stockroom boy were to bale up all the waste paper and cardboard for the war effort, and to keep the place tidy. The only mechanical aid was a hand-operated press that the wires could be passed through, and then hand-knotted to secure the bale. These then had to be manoeuvred by hand – walked or wheeled on a sack-truck. Each bale weighed about two hundredweight and they had to be stacked up to at least four high, to save space, then loaded onto the lorry by hand. It kept me very fit indeed.

The other work included helping to unload deliveries, unpacking and checking the content, packing away stock on appropriate shelves and re-stocking the showroom contents. Some goods didn't need to be carried up to the stockroom, they were so scarce during the war that they went straight out on to the counters and all were sold within an hour or so. People were willing to queue halfway up the High Street before we even got them unloaded. Things like torch and cycle batteries, and enamel saucepans were of the highest priority.

The showroom floor needed to be swept several times a day with a broom that was about two feet wide; our customers had to watch out if they didn't want a sore ankle. On Saturday nights after the last customer had left, the floor had to be thoroughly swept, before treating it with linseed oil and leaving it to dry over the weekend. The main showroom lights also had to be cleaned regularly. It was a never-ending job, I remember the tall steps that I used were very shaky and liable to collapse at any time. Stoking up the central heating boiler with coke, and cleaning out the clinker, was another task during the winter months. This took up a lot of time; it was hot, dirty and smelly with noxious fumes. Some of the girls had to do this job before I arrived, so they were quite pleased when I appeared on the scene. The modern equivalent of stockroom boy is a trainee manager. I wonder if today's 14-year-old would be willing to do all I was expected to do, and be happy doing it?

All the shop staff wore maroon overalls, Supervisors had smarter blue overalls, and stockroom staff were issued with khaki-coloured overalls. The manageress, Miss Thompson, was a wonderful person, firm and strict but totally fair. She did have most of us in tears from time to time, but in my case I definitely deserved her wrath. I was caught taking things without paying, and she dealt with me strongly but privately. I would often find myself riding to work with her, as our cycle paths joined at about the halfway point. She always seemed to welcome my company. Unfortunately within two years she died of tuberculosis. My mother had predicted this when she read her teacup, but of course never told her or anyone at the time.

Aunt Vera, the cook, liked to hold 'wild' parties at her home at 77 Spencer Avenue. Everyone was invited: most of the younger Woolworth's girls and myself, my friends and any Woolworth's customers who wanted to join in, especially the servicemen who were away from home. The living room floor would be cleared and polished for dancing, the Console Radiogram volume would be turned up, and the glasses lined up ready for the drinks brought by the revellers. The Inkspots, Bing Crosby, Victor Sylvester and the Andrew Sisters were all the rage in those days. What a time we had! We had to be prepared to walk or ride home on our bikes afterwards of course; the last bus would have gone, and it would be pitch-black because strict blackout regulations would be in force. One of the regulars who always came when on leave was an RAF ground mechanic working on Spitfires for the Eagle Squadron. This squadron comprised of volunteer American fighter pilots, who joined the RAF to get into the fight during the Battle of Britain. This was long before America came into the war officially. Their base was often shot up and bombed by the Luftwaffe, and many of his friends were killed. he survived the war but was killed soon after demob, in a motorcycle accident on Station Bridge, Scunthorpe.

When I was 15, I fell in love with Nadine Mitchell, who I called 'Flash' for some reason. We were good friends, but I don't think my passion was reciprocated. Remember Sandy Sanderson, who had recognised me as the boy who stole stamps off her counter? There was a sad follow-up to that. Sandy was talking to a sailor for rather a long time at her counter one day, which was not allowed. The manageress asked the sailor to leave, and gave Sandy a good telling-off. It was Sandy's brother and he was lost

Picture: Des Whitby

Des Whitby, pictured when he left the store at Scunthorpe in 1945 in order to become a trainee radio engineer

with his ship the following day. We were all sad about this. One day in the staff canteen, we were messing about and I pulled a chair from under her, causing her to fall rather heavily. This was a silly thing for me to do: I never did apologise, but I am apologising now (a bit late, perhaps, but I mean it).

The stock delivery drivers were not really staff, but we did see them often and got to know them quite well. One was from Grimsby and he had been an RAF pilot during WWI. In the early part of the war he told us that if they spotted a German plane over the trenches, they would just wave and wish them well. Later on however, they started throwing bricks and other missiles, graduating to pistols, rifles and finally to machine-guns as the war developed. There was also a lady driver, who delivered goods from the local railway depot.

Her van was very old: crash gears, an open-fronted cab, and only a canvas cover to protect her legs. She said that after driving a van like that for a few years, she was frightened to go back to riding a bike.

Woolworth's Café Bar was a meeting place on an international scale. There were servicemen from South Africa, Australia, Canada, New Zealand, America, Poland, Czechoslovakia, France, Holland, Belgium and Britain. It was standing room only, always busy from opening to closing time. Buttered rolls and Horlicks are what I remember best – both scarce during the war and considered a rare luxury by all of our customers. The airmen were a particularly cheerful, happy-go-lucky lot, mostly bomber aircrews based at the local airfields. They would come in after a night out over enemy-occupied territory, ready to relax and have a cup of tea in friendly company and chat up the girls. Many we did not see again; when asked about them, their friends would say 'oh! he bought it last night, we saw them go down in flames'. They couldn't afford to be too upset about this because they still had to go out again the following night.

The young railway lads were regular customers, mainly to chat up the girls if the manageress wasn't about. They were employed as engine-cleaners to begin with, then progressed to firemen and eventually drivers. One of them, Graham Wells, became my brother-in-law after courting and marrying my sister. Two strange characters in civilian clothing, who claimed to be Secret Service Agents, were on-and-off visitors. Apparently they went in and out of occupied Europe by MTB or submarine to carry out various subversive missions, working mostly with the 'Underground'. One day they came in looking tired and roughed up, saying that the previous night they were 'blown' and only escaped after a 'shootout' with the Gestapo in Amsterdam. A tall story perhaps, but they were both accepted as genuine by the servicemen at the bar.'

Des Whitby

No plastic gloves here

'In the Twickenham store I was occasionally moved across to the biscuit counter, where the biscuits were not sold in packets but weighed out of large tins. One of the most popular tins with the less-well-off families was the one containing broken biscuits. I don't remember us being particularly concerned about hygiene in those days – there were no plastic gloves'.

Carol Annelay

'I was here first!'

'The first branch of Woolworth's I worked in was at Borehamwood in Hertfordshire. My aunt, Elsie Weller, was a supervisor at the store and she got me the job. There was no interview, as far as I remember: I just turned up and was introduced to the manager, Mr Fellows, a tall, slim man with red hair. My wages were to be £7 10s a week: this was in 1961. My aunt was one of three supervisors, the other two being Mrs Curtis and Chris World, and they all wore button-through overalls in dark blue; the rest of us wore overalls of pale turquoise. Each morning we would go upstairs to the staff cloakroom, don our overalls, hang up our coats and put our belongings in a locker before all trooping downstairs to our respective departments. Adjacent to the cloakroom there was a sickroom with a bed and we would be sent up there if we were feeling unwell during working hours.

Most departments in the store consisted of a rectangular island with counters on each of the four sides. The staff would stand in the middle of the island, and there was one till on each of the four sides. The stock on the flat counters was divided by glass partitions with a glass panel at the front. The customers would stand anywhere around the island and wait for us to come to them. Sometimes when the store was busy, it was difficult to remember who had been waiting to be served the longest. Often, irate customers would tap repeatedly on the glass shouting 'Miss, Miss, I was here first': it could be very annoying. Besides the islands there were departments along most of the walls as well, and these had one till each. Every afternoon one girl from each department would write out a list of the stock she needed to replenish the counters, and go up to the stockroom with it. Fast-selling items were kept below the counters to fill up during the morning. This was known as 'understock' and was only accessible from the rear of the counter.

The first department I worked in was grocery, which was located along one of the walls as you entered the store. Nearest the door was a chiller cabinet, then the till, followed by shelving reaching from the floor to just above head height. Butter, margarine, lard and milk were kept in the chiller cabinet. On the shelves we stocked tinned food, jams and dry goods such as sugar, flour, baking powder, bicarbonate of soda, dried fruits, cereals, suet and tea. Everytime something was sold from the shelves, the goods behind had to be pulled forward to make the shelves look full.

This was called 'fronting up'.

The tills were mechanical and seem very primitive today. Each of the keys on the till had a different number on it, and you keyed in the amount in pounds, shillings and pence. The amount then popped up in a little window at the top. When the sale was complete, the customer would hand over their cash, you'd press a key to open the till drawer, take the change out, and push the drawer shut. The tills didn't tell us how much change to give – we had to work it out in our head – and no receipt was ever produced. It was mostly coins in the 1960s with just the occasional £1 note. You could buy an awful lot for a pound. All the change had to be counted out into the customer's hand, starting from the total amount of the sale up to the amount tendered. Security was non-existent, as most of the time when the drawer was open, our back was turned to the customer. If we made a mistake with the amount of change, we would just press the 'no sale' key and the drawer would come out again for us to rectify our mistake. There were no locks on the tills, so there was nothing to stop anyone pressing 'no sale' and stealing the contents.

I was only in grocery for a short time before being moved to drapery, where I stayed for the next few years. The grey-haired lady I worked with was called Ivy Sewell and she must have been the oldest member of staff at the time. The layout of our department was a bit different to the others as it had a frame built around the top, so we could display some of our stock on coat hangers. This frame was high above our heads and we had to get the goods down using a long pole with a hook on the end. The frame displayed trousers, skirts, blouses, jumpers, overalls and nighties, and on the counter we sold aprons, pinafores, vest, pants, bras and cotton handkerchiefs. Some of the best-selling items at that time were baby-doll pyjamas and nightdress cases in the shape of poodles. These came in black, white and grey.

Another department I helped out in was haberdashery. In the 1960s many women still made or knitted garments for their families and the goods sold on this counter reflected this. Knitting wool and needles were sold along with crochet hooks. Wool was ordered and kept under the counter for customers who couldn't afford to purchase it all at once. They would come in each week to buy a bit more until their garment was complete. Knitting patterns and paper dressmaking patterns also sold well. Other items were buttons (sold loose and on cards), safety pins, needles, hooks and eyes, zips and cottons. The cottons came in many colours and the reels were made of wood. The haberdashery counter was also where you would buy sanitary towels and tampons.

The other departments were interesting, though I never served on them. I remember on electrical seeing a selection of torches for sale along with loose batteries and bulbs. Light bulbs came in packets with no base so each one could be tested in front of the customer to check they worked. This was done by screwing or pushing them into a contraption on the counter until they lit up. All batteries were tested by inserting them into a device with a small bulb attached. Wire and cable came on large reels and was sold by the yard. A brass measuring stick was attached to the counter. Above the island in this department was a false ceiling, where different lampshades were displayed. My friend Eve Cousins, who worked in electrical, said it was hot standing beneath them all day.

Another friend, Joan Western, worked on sweets, where sweets and chocolates were sold in bars and tubes from the flat counter. These included Woolies own brand of chocolate called Melba, which tasted awful. A boiled sweet called Spangles was popular at this time, as were Wagon Wheels which have shrunk considerably over the years. Sherbet dips always sold well, with their liquorice straw inside. Penny and ha'penny sweets were sold loose, such as Trebor chews, flying saucers and gobstoppers. The counter also sold salted peanuts and cashew nuts, hot from a machine, and Smiths crisps which came only in plain flavour with a tiny bit of salt contained in a twist of blue paper loose in the bag.

Records in those days were all 45rpm, made of vinyl and came in a paper sleeve. I think they sold the Top 20 but what I remember were the cover versions, which were sung by unknown artists. These were much cheaper and were issued on Woolies' own label called Embassy. Woolworth's always had a good display of fountain pens, bottles of blue or black ink, pencils, wax crayons, and wooden pencil boxes with a sliding lid. There was always a wide selection of notepaper and envelopes, as letter writing was very popular. Colouring and magic painting books always sold well, as did books of cut-out dolls. We also sold used foreign postage stamps, as stamp collecting was a popular hobby with both boys and girls. The stamps came in little packets from either a single country or mixed. Stamp hinges and tweezers and a number of stamp albums were also available. Other albums sold were for photographs, and triangular adhesive corners were sold in packets to attach the photos to the pages.

My friend Pauline Wheatley worked in the hardware department which was along the wall at the back of the store. All sorts of pots and pans were sold at one end along with bowls, basins, china and tea-sets. The other end was where you would find brooms, brush and dustpans and plastic washing-up bowls.

On the ground floor, just past the grocery department, were doors that led to the first floor and to the office, which was on mezzanine level. Past these doors was the goods lift that went up to the stockroom. Staff were not allowed to travel in the lift but had to use the stairs. The lift itself was about 15ft square and had two sliding doors. First to be closed was an inner metal gate, followed by a concertina-shaped outer door. It was an unwritten rule that if anyone left the doors open at either end, you would bang on the metal door in front of you, which could be heard on the other floor. Someone would then rush to close the doors enabling you to call the lift. Heating in the stockroom was non-existent, which wasn't very nice when we were stocktaking in January. One of my most vivid memories from that time was when Mr Fellows would bring us steaming hot cups of Bovril to warm us up. The staff canteen was upstairs and that's where we took our morning and afternoon breaks. At lunchtime it served hot meals for a shilling. Meal times were staggered and I always tried to get the same times as my friends Even, Joan and Pauline, because on summer days we would often go up onto the flat roof of the store to enjoy the sunshine'.

Jean Croft

Gossip in the alleyway

'I started as a Saturday girl at Woolworth's in Broadmead, Bristol, selling pots, pans, cutlery, plastic bowls, bins and metal dustbins, earning 11s 9d for a 9am-6pm day. During the school holidays I worked full time and when I left school in 1967, I went to work elsewhere as a trainee supervisor.

The Woolworth's store was a long rectangular one with a front entrance in Broadmead and a back entrance in Fairfax Street, opposite the large new Co-operative department store 'Fairfax House'. It had the standard wooden 'enclosed' rectangular counters and no-one was allowed to leave the counters without permission. We were also not permitted to sit down – the supervisors (in their navy overalls) swooped on any that did.

I was lucky enough to work at one of the sloping pyramid counters along the side wall at the back of the store. The goods were stacked on shelves and hooks on a partition about 30 inches out from the wall, with a small alcove space between sections. This space contained a till, a pull-out wooden flap to rest the goods on while you cashed or wrapped them up, and a pull-down round wooden disc. This was to sit on at the end of the day, even though you were not allowed to do so. There was also a roll of brown wrapping paper. I could wander up and down the section at will to 'organise' the shelves (in other words, chat to the girls on the counters alongside.) The space between the partition and the wall formed an alleyway where there was a sink in which I could wash my hands. At quiet times the alleyway was very busy with staff washing hands and catching up on gossip. I also remember one Christmas the male floorwalker using it to give female counter staff a Merry Christmas kiss!

We stocked a myriad of kitchen odds and ends. The dustbins were stored on a shelf about eight feet off the ground. We had no steps and got very good at standing on a lower shelf and tipping them forward and catching them for the customer. Next to the hardware was the china section. All the crockery and hardware was sold individually and priced accordingly. Couples saving to get married or those newly wed, bought one or two items a week as they could afford them, until they had a full set. I got to know a lot of customers by name as they came in each week. All items had to be added up in your head and the total price entered into the 'plunger' type tills. This was a mammoth task when customers often bought full teasets and sets of pans and tools for wedding presents.

You had to bang the plungers on the till down hard or they would stick. All the items had to be individually wrapped in brown paper, no easy task with large items and the small working space on the pull-out flap, and often with a crowd of people waiting to be served and giving advice. I learned all the tricks of wrapping quickly and still to this day wrap everything efficiently in double-quick time. I had to wear a dull green wrap-over nylon overall that never fitted, whatever your shape or size. We all complained about them and wanted the cream button ones that were much more modern and worn only by the staff serving food.

Everyone was very friendly and there was a real feeling of community. We all helped each other out, covering sections while staff went to collect stock. Staff on each counter made out stock lists for the warehouse staff, on the top floor of the building, and they would send down the goods in the lifts in large wicker crates on wheels. These would be left by the lifts on the sales floor for the section staff to collect and put out on shelves. The crates were heavy and always had wobbly wheels that never ran straight. Invariably stock was missing or ran out during the day and I'd have to go upstairs to the warehouse to collect stock myself when few customers were about.

The offices and clocking on-off machine were on the first floor. There was only one old machine for the whole store and always congestion around it at the start and end of the day. Woe betide anyone caught clocking on or off for groups of friends as well as themselves.

There was also a mezzanine floor with a very well-used customer café that served steak and kidney pie cut from very large catering trays. Chips were served with everything. The food was reasonably priced and very popular, especially on a Saturday.

I really enjoyed the time I worked at the store as it seemed we were always laughing, although we worked very hard and always had aching legs by the end of the day. Many years later the Broadmead store was modernised and eventually demolished when the 'Galleries' was built, but I have very fond memories of it and the great women I met working there.

The pay wasn't great and the store tended to be staffed by those who did not have much and patronised by customers who couldn't afford a lot. This led to quite a unique atmosphere.'

Cathy Howard

Accidental bonus

'I remember being 'promoted' to the loose biscuits counter in the Cardigan store and serving my first customer. He wanted one 1 lb of loose biscuits so, placing the weights on one side of the scales and the biscuits on the other, I weighed it all very nervously and bagged the biscuits. It was only after the customer had gone that I noticed that I had put a 2 lb weight on the scales, and he had himself a bargain.'

Ethne Biggs

Vinegar and water

'I worked in Weston-Super-Mare 50 years ago and was on the babywear counter. We had our own till and Terry's nappies were 2s 6d each. We had to wash our wooden counters with vinegar and water at least once a week. Then I did holiday relief work and this took me to many different departments: there was ladies' and men's underwear and swimwear, which was laid out flat on the counter and had to be kept tidy at all times; then the sweet counter – we would pinch a sweet and duck under the counter to eat it – and finally the tea-bar, where sandwiches were made and tea and coffee sold. There were only two stools, so all the rest of the customers had to stand up. There were three entrances – one on the High Street, a side entrance and one at the rear of the store leading to North Street.'

Patricia Hodge

Mis-shapes were a bargain

'My mum worked in Gosport Woolworth's for a while on the sweet counter. She used to bring home the mis-shapes, sometimes those chocolate buttons with the hundreds and thousands on top, or sometimes just mis-shapen chocolates. We were quite hard up and she was saving up to meet dad, as his ship was due to dock for a couple of weeks in southern Spain, opposite Gibraltar.'

Patricia Roberts

A hot lunch for a shilling

'Before leaving school in 1963, I attempted to obtain an office job, as I was having private lessons for shorthand and typing. Having 'no experience of office work', I was unsuccessful. So I went for an interview at Woolworth's instead and landed a job at the Didcot store working in the stockroom.

Didcot was a brilliant place with its own staff canteen. The meals were cooked by Mrs Bishop and were well balanced, just like school dinners with a meat or fish dish, vegetables, potatoes and a pudding. They also cost the same – one shilling.

Although I did not keep my first wage slip, I made a note of it: it was £3.8s 5d. Out of this, I gave my parents £1.10s a week towards my keep and spent the rest on records, visits to the cinema or going to Oxford for the day (plus putting some aside for savings).

My job in the stockroom entailed pricing goods that arrived by road and rail. Staff checked in the goods, then passed them to me for pricing for which I used a hand-held machine. Sometimes the sales floor below were waiting for items that were out of stock, so these were checked through quickly. Saturday girls helped me with pricing, especially when we had a lot of goods in.

As time progressed and the check-in staff were on holiday or off sick, I became responsible for checking in the goods from road and rail, placing them in the lift to go up to the stockroom ready to be priced. I enjoyed the responsibility of this and the manual work involved. The store must have been ahead of its time as it had a bailing machine, where all the cardboard boxes, after being emptied of goods (soap powder ones held about 48 packets) were loaded in the machine, compacted and collected weekly.

Six months before I left, I went on the sales floor, where the goods I looked after were toys and houseware. The store was open Monday to Saturday, with half-day closing on Wednesday. Out of

Picture: Ann McKinley

Modernisation for Woolworth's in Didcot with the opening of its new self-service store on Thursday 6 September 1956

my wages I put away 10 shillings a week. I was able to put a deposit on a brand new three-speed Triumph bicycle in September 1963, which cost £25 5s. My parents entered a hire purchase agreement with Bosleys, a local shop, and I gave them the money for this each week. After this had been paid off, I started saving a deposit for an Olivetti typewriter, so that I could get more typing practice for office employment. This I purchased in March 1964 for £28 10s from W H Smith.

On the day of Sir Winston Churchill's funeral, the shop closed from 11am – 12 noon and staff listened to it on the radio.

The manager during my time at Woolworth's was Fred Butolph. He was fair and when I left, he said if it didn't work out for me I could always go back. I cannot recall when the store closed in Didcot. Mr Butolph went onto other stores and managed the large Woolworth's in Cornmarket, Oxford. Sadly this closed in 1982 and he had the task of telling the staff. I always look back fondly and with pride to my days at Woolworth's. I was fortunate that my first job gave me the experience of working in a shop, both behind the scenes in the stores and also serving customers on the shop floor.'

Ann McKinley

Popping the lightbulbs

'My best friend and I were both waiting for Civil Service appointments, but had to find work in the meantime. There was no such thing as benefits until you had six months' worth of Insurance stamps. We started at Woolworth's Cosham, Portsmouth, branch in 1958 as shop assistants. I lived at the other end of the city, so cycled four or five miles to work every day. My wages were £3 a week gross; after National Insurance it came to £2 15s 4d.

The branch was an old-fashioned one divided into two sections. My friend Pat was lucky enough to work on the make-up counter in the smarter part of the store, while I was posted in the gloomy old part on the electrical counter. We had to test light bulbs before we sold them by plugging them into a little machine and pressing a switch. Unfortunately if you didn't press the switch exactly right, the bulb popped. After popping several bulbs, the exasperated assistant decided she wouldn't let me do this any more.

One time I was put on the plant counter for the day. We sold hyacinths in glass bowls, the idea being that you didn't need soil, just water. We had one displayed on the counter as a demonstration. It was growing nicely, so when a dear old lady asked if she could buy that one, I sold it to her. When the other assistant saw it had gone, she went bananas as it had been earmarked for the manager.'

Jan Grinham

Crumbs everywhere

'When other departments became very busy in the Borehamwood store, us girls were moved around to help out for a while. I remember often being sent to help Mrs Hoddinott on biscuits. All the familiar biscuits were sold loose by weight, not in packets. Each variety was contained in a tin about 15 inches square. One tin always contained broken biscuits, which were cheaper. The customer would buy the biscuits by the pound and could either choose a single variety or a pound of mixed. We used our bare hands to take the biscuits out of the tin and place them into a paper bag. All the crumbs would get under our fingernails. The bag of biscuits was then placed into a bowl on the weighing scales and a weight was placed on the other side. Biscuits were added or removed until the scales balanced. When removed, the bag was held by the corners and flipped over a couple of times to secure it. Money changed hands but I don't remember ever washing my hands between sales.'

Jean Croft

Friday night is Amami night

'At Woolworth's in Leicester, at Gallowtree Gate, I was employed not by the store but by a popular cosmetics house – Outdoor Girl/Miners – and received my weekly wage from them by post. My starting wage in 1959 was around £6 per week plus commission. This was excellent considering my age, and considerably more than the Woolworth's girls were earning. It was a happy time for me doing something that I was interested in.

I wore a pink nylon overall with the company name embroidered on: this was unique and probably came about because the owners of the cosmetic company were American. The Woolworth's staff wore maroon cotton overalls, and the food department staff wore white cotton and cap. My duties were to sell and advise on the use of various products including lipsticks and mascara which came in three different forms – block, cream and a (revolutionary) wand type. Lipsticks were 1s 6d, with larger sizes in gold cases at 2s 6d. We had a lot of items stolen on Saturdays due to the store being very busy.

In the 1950s and 60s there was a popular saying: 'Friday night is Amami Night' – and this was certainly true in Leicester. At that time the city had a huge manufacturing industry, making knitwear, underwear, hosiery, boots and shoes. These giant factories employed large numbers of women who had money to spend on themselves, and spend it they did.

The factories usually finished around 4.30pm on Friday, and then the girls used to pour into Woolworth's to buy shampoos, Amami setting lotion, and small bottles of perfume such as Phul Nana, Californian Poppy, June, Evening in Paris, Ashes of Roses and Ashes of Violets. Cosmetics (or 'mek up' in Leicester lingo) were in abundance with so many brands available: Ponds, Snowfire, Tangee, Outdoor Girl and Miners, Diana Marsh and Betty Lou. All were popular and inexpensive brands in Woolworth's so the girls would buy a different colour each week. We certainly had lots of 'regulars' and for about a pound, you could buy all you needed. The toiletries section also sold sundries such as mirrors, sponges, powder puffs, nail files, hair grips and slides. Each week there were new additions to the range and some exciting, fresh items being introduced. The last half-hour of the day was spent doing a general tidy-up and re-stock ready for the following morning. This is when we found the empty cards that the goods had been taken from.

Leicester had several city centre cinemas in the 50s, 60s and 70s. Closest to Woolworth's Gallowtree Gate store were The Picture House, Gaumont and The Odeon. Apart from ice-cream, nowhere offered much in the way of sweets and confectionery so Woolworth's was the place to go to buy before going to the matinee. What a joy the sweet counter in Woolworth's was. Almost all sweets were sold loose, without boxes or wrappers, and all were weighed up for you in a polished brass scale pan. Such delights as Blue Bird toffees, Palm Toffee, Parkinson's butterscotch, Needlers fruit drops, Everton Mints, Foxes Glacier Mints, Clarnico mint creams and Regency selection (these were a mixture of soft candy fondants, jellies and chocolates, liquorice All Sorts, Pontefract Cakes and coconut mushrooms). My own favourites were Roses and Violets; these were dark chocolates with mauve or pink fondant centres and topped with a tiny piece of crystallised petal, They were about 1s 9d for a quarter – quite expensive at the time.

The sweet counter also had a heated hotplate that sold roasted nuts, peanuts and cashew nuts. They always smelt very appetising and were all weighed out by the quarter. It was to be many years before Spangles pre-wrapped boiled sweets came in. They were very popular with such varieties as fruits, mints, Old English, butterscotch, acid drops and many more. And at 3d a tube you could afford to have more than one.'

Jennifer Lymn

Fireworks spark romance

'I started on the make-up and toiletries counter at Woolworth's in Fishergate, Preston, in the summer of 1955, selling Miners lipstick and Bourjois rouge. The counters were long, narrow wooden affairs; we walked up and down in the centre of them feeling like the captain of a boat. At Christmas, the store would be so packed with shoppers that it took ages to battle our way through (from the safety of the counters) to get to our breaks.

Picture: Dorothy Byers

Dorothy Byers (left) with her window-dressing tutor Miss Spall. They are pictured in 1958 outside the store in Fishergate, Preston, where Dorothy had just finished the display for Baby Week

I also eventually became the window dresser and went on a week's course at Blackpool to learn how to do them. I met Harry, my future husband, while I was making a window display for firework night. He was with someone I knew, and they were pulling funny faces at me through the window while I was working on the display.

We got married in 1962 and I left Woolies in 1963 when I was pregnant. I used to spend my dinner-times knitting baby clothes in the canteen. So, as you can imagine, I have some fond memories of Woolworth's and my time there, which led to a very happy marriage. I have also been a frequent shopper there: I still have a complete boxed teaset, the box stamped with 'F W Woolworth's Golden Jubilee', and also two of the staff magazines called *New Bond.'*

Dorothy Byers

Picture: Dorothy Byers

The busy frontage of the store in Fishergate, Preston

My dates with Pete were a secret

'I spent a total of 42 years with Woolworth's, joining back in 1959 when I left school. My first three months were spent at a very old, tiny store, with high wooden counters that I could not see over to serve the customers: it was store no. 226 at Loughborough. A new store was being built across the road in the Market Place and we moved across in the summer. It was a lovely shop and I was given the fancy goods department, the birthday cards and the small record section where we sold singles under the Embassy Label (I still have some I bought in the 1960s).

In 1961 a new trainee manager called Pete arrived at the store and he asked me out to the cinema. We were not supposed to go out with anyone working at the store, so we had to keep it quiet. Nevertheless, the romance continued and we married in 1964. After I'd given birth to my son, I returned to Woolworth's in 1972.

We had some good times but it was also hard work. To order stock, we counted up our stock and wrote the amount you required in the department's binder. This went up to the office, where order-forms were filled in. Only then would you be able to have the stock.

We sold everything from screws to biscuits, and each Monday the first job was to do our checking lists.

I held various positions over the years – first I was a sales assistant, then a supervisor, then section manager. I was given the chance to apply for assistant manager. After taking the test, I was offered a post at store no. 474 at Coalville and moved there in August 1992. At first I found it so different, but the team was just as nice and I stayed until 2008. We were like a family who looked out for each other.'

Lila Walker

Respect, honesty and hard work

'When we moved to Shropshire in 1961 I managed to get a job at Woolies in Wellington as a shop assistant. It was very strict but I enjoyed my time there. Because of my husband's job, we moved to Kidderminster and I got a seasonal job on the Christmas card counter there. The staff were very nice and made sure we had our lunch breaks and ate something, because some of the girls fainted as they had been standing all day. My third Woolworth's job was at the Winson Green branch in Birmingham, where I worked in the canteen looking after the girls' meal-break. The cook there was a lovely lady by the name of Mrs Morgan. They were good times: there was respect, honesty, and we were not afraid of hard work.'

Ivy Leonard

Saturday treats

'As a young girl back in 1955-56 I worked full time in Cosham near Portsmouth. Not having a lot of money in those days, my two sisters and brother always looked forward to the loose broken biscuits mum used to buy us, as they often included cream ones and those pink wafers. That was our one treat on a Saturday.'

Pamela Poate

Peanut parlour

'My friend Elaine Smith and I worked on the loose biscuit counter at the Woolworth's store in Arnside Road, Southmead, Bristol in 1952. On the biscuit counter we also had a hot-peanut dispenser. They were kept hot by means of a light bulb and were very popular with customers'.

Jean Ford

Keeping the store spick and span

'After I left school in 1962 I decided to work for a local building company. After six months I was taken on as apprentice painter, decorator and general maintenance hand and was bound to the company for five years with day-release to college. The company worked for several large stores and had a maintenance contract with Woolworth's in the Portsmouth area.

Our main store was the Commercial Road branch, where we had to look out for any woodworm and dry rot, because the sales counters were made of wood. On Wednesday afternoons, when the store was closed, we also had to clean out the two grease traps situated on the sales floor directly under the cafeteria kitchen.

The internal plumbing came down through a false pillar and

Picture: Jean Ford

Picture: Elaine Smith

Jean Ford (right) and Elaine Smith in their 'biscuit counter' uniforms at the store in Arnside Road, Southmead, Bristol in 1952

Members of the Southmead, Bristol, store setting off on an outing in the 1950s

the traps were covered by a number of wooden covers and plinths, all of which had to be removed to gain access. Firstly we cleared the grease traps, decanted the foul water into a large galvanised dustbin and took it away. When we had finished, we sprayed water and disinfectant around the traps, re-sealed them and replaced the flooring covers. After this task we were allowed a 15-minute smoke break. We then returned to check the inside of the wooden counters. This was quite an awkward job because we had to crawl along the narrow walkways using a torch to inspect for woodworm and dry rot.

During my five years nothing was found, possibly due to the fact that these counters were made of hardwood. The only damage was to the plinths due to general wear and tear, being bumped by prams, merchandising trolleys, boots and shoes. We always carried with us several lengths of wooden plinths made by our own workshop if replacements were needed.

All the counters were numbered and checked on a rolling maintenance schedule. We also had other routine jobs: checking around the store for any damage, such as broken windows, and cleaning out the front door hinge-mechanism so that dust did not accumulate. We would also wash and clean the fascia boards and signs, removing each gold letter for easy access. They were quite dirty because in those days Commercial Road was the main access to the city. If the letters were dropped, they chipped and the gold leaf was easily damaged. Any repair to these was very expensive. Any wear and tear to the fascia board was repaired and if the paintwork required touching up, it received two coats of red gloss paint.

Eventually it was decided that it was better to remove all the shop-front fascia boards so that they could be painted, repaired and gilded in the workshop. It took two weeks to carry out the work and Woolworth's were very strict as to the specification. It had to be seven coats of Valspar paint – one primer, three undercoats, two gloss and one of clear varnish. When finished they were immaculate.

Every five years the whole interior of the sales floor, ceiling and walls were painted. All work had to be carried out during the night after the store closed at 5.30pm. We had scaffolding erected across the complete width of the store and worked our way from back to front, applying two coats of white satin-finish paint. Smoking was allowed when working on site. Six to eight painters worked all night and it took us six weeks to complete.

We stopped work at five in the morning, took down the scaffolding, removed dustsheets from the counters and generally cleared up. After the ceiling was finished, the walls and pillars were painted in a colour called 'sales floor pink', applied by roller.

After this refurbishment, we used to do day-work, painting the staff area and corridors and doing general maintenance. We always got on well with the staff and managers and I recollect that in those days we all saw the store manager, who thanked us and praised us for our work.

One time, I was taking a plumber round the store to find a blocked pipe. It was located in one of the pillars. We inspected it and took off the cover, only to be confronted with a loud gurgling then a jet of water which fired across almost the whole length of the store, narrowly missing several astonished customers.'

Peter Taylor

The tale of the penny apple

'I took a lot of pride in my displays on the fruit counter, polishing the apples until they shone and then stacking them in a pyramid for display. I'd been put in charge of the counter when I joined Woolworth's in Cosham High Street, Portsmouth, in 1959, along with my cousin Patty. There was one lady who came to my counter every Friday evening after I had set my display up for the next day and would insist on buying apples from my display and not from the back. I told her that all the apples were the same and that I would never sell her anything I wouldn't eat myself, I also told her that if I ever sold her rotten fruit, she could bring it back and make me eat it in front of her. Still she insisted that she wanted them from my display. So, through gritted teeth, I would give her what she wanted and watch my hard work go to waste. The worst part was that she enjoyed watching me do it because she stood there smiling all the time.

Another memory which still makes me laugh is the time Patty decided to help me at the end of the day, taking all the waste fruit and vegetables out to the bin. I told her to wait for me so I could guide her through the pathway that I'd made through all the wooden boxes and crates that were out in the yard. It was very dark out there and I didn't want her hurting herself. Patty, with an air of self-confidence, said 'I'll be all right' and didn't wait for me. As I started out with my load, I heard a very loud crash: Patty was flat on her back using some not very ladylike language. I took one look at her and couldn't stop laughing, my sides ached: she looked so funny with all the boxes and stinky fruit scattered around her and she was screaming at me to help her. The only damage was a few bruises. Now she laughs with me when we talk about it.

One of my memories of working in Woolworth's was when I was standing next to the entrance to my counter and talking to one of the managers when we both noticed a sixpence on the floor. I looked at my boss and said: 'am I right in saying that if that sixpence is on the inside of the counter it is yours, and if it's on the outside of the counter it's mine?' 'Yes,' he said. I then kicked the sixpence clear of the counter and said 'then I guess it is mine.' He laughed and let me keep it.

I think my favourite memory is of a small boy who looked like he could do with a good feed. He came to my counter with a penny in his hand and asked me if I had a penny apple. Of course I found him a really nice one, and you would have thought I had given him a pot of gold. He became a regular customer, always asking for a penny apple. It was years later when I had left Woolworth's to work in a factory, that one day I saw a young man sweeping the factory floor. When our eyes met, we recognised each other and he said: 'do you remember the penny apple?' I felt like I had met an old friend and knew that we had made a memory that we would never forget.'

Anita Hancock

Picture: Kath Trace

Sisters Kath, Dot and Brenda Lawson all worked at Woolworth's in Cosham, Portsmouth, in the 1940s and are pictured here with some of the other girls

The New Bond

The House Journal of F. W. Woolworth and Co., Limited

Vol. 30   No. 3   June/July, 1971

The New Bond, the magazine for Woolworth's UK employees.
This issue is from June/July 1971

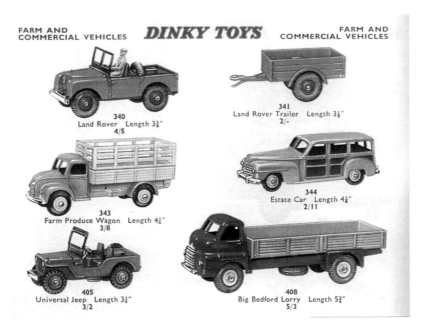

The 'farm and commercial vehicles' page of the Dinky Toy catalogue of the 1950s. A farm produce wagon was 3s 8d and an estate car cost 2s 11d

The cover of an Extended Play record on the Embassy label, sold exclusively in Woolworth's: this one contains 'vocal gems' from Gigi and Kismet. Picture courtesy of Brian Robinson

Argyle Street in Glasgow pictured in 1950 or 1951, with Woolworth's just visible between the two trams. Picture courtesy of STTS

The East Street, Bridport store in Dorset. Not only has Woolworth's vanished from our High Streets, but the Ford Anglia in the foreground is now a collectors' item

Woolworth's Knitting Magazine for 1973 featured 99 pages of knitting and crochet patterns and was a bargain at 14p. Woolworth's also stocked a complete range of wool, needles and accessories

Kleeware dolls-house furniture sold by Woolworth's after the Second World War. Picture courtesy of Joy Matthews

Woolworth's jewellery including a flying-duck brooch and a 'pearl' necklace. Picture courtesy of Joy Matthews

A fine summer day in Ledbury in the 1960s. The Morris 1000 on the right is just pulling away from the front of Woolworth's

The Woolworth's building in New York. When it opened in 1913 it was the tallest building in the world

The Woolworth's Christmas tree bought for 65p by Ethel Phillips in the Yeovil store during the 1970s. The tree is still used each Christmas, and is topped with a 1950s Woolworth's fairy. Picture courtesy of The Western Gazette

Treasured memories: the two china dogs bought by Paula Perry's mother in the
Weymouth store in 1935 or 1936. As a child, Paula was allowed to hold the
dogs, but only while sitting down – and only on a Sunday.
Picture courtesy of Paula Perry

Still in use despite several house-moves is this Royal Vale bone china tea-set,
made by Ridgway Potteries and bought by Derek and Pam Phillips in July 1964
from the Frome branch of Woolworth's

Commemorative Yearbook issued in 1999 for the 90th anniversary of the opening of the first store in Great Britain, and containing photographs of the directors and managers of the company

A mint example of the Coronation Coach made by Lesney Products
and sold through Woolworth's.
Picture courtesy of Kevin McGimpsey of the Matchbox Club

Shopper Sandra Pritcher stands amid the empty shelving during the last hour of
trading at the Exmouth store, 5 January 2009. Picture courtesy of Nick Diprose

Customers flock to the store in Marine place, Seaton, East Devon, for its last day
of trading. Woolworth's had served the population there for 55 years.
Picture courtesy of David Morgan

SATURDAY GIRLS AND BOYS

Too young for make-up

'It was almost a rite of passage to get a Saturday job to buy stockings, lipstick and records. Parents would not buy stockings or lipstick as, at 14, we were judged too young for such things. I passed my arithmetic test and started at Woolies in Erith, Kent in 1968. I was given my overall and taken behind the counter, which was all wood. The cash till was shiny, made of white metal and brass. My first wage packet was a small brown envelope containing 12 shillings and six pence. When I became 15 it went up to 15 shillings. We had a staff canteen, which served lovely food – shepherd's pie and steamed pudding with custard. Nothing fancy, just good British food at a very reasonable price. In our afternoon break, we had currant buns loaded with butter.'

Stella Smart

Mental arithmetic

'In 1950, when I was 15, I worked as a Saturday girl in the West Ealing branch of Woolworth's. I was good at mental arithmetic so I coped well with adding up the cost of two or four ounces of various sweets plus the price of chocolate bars. At the same time I had to total the number of ration-book points required and cut them out from the customer's books. All went well for several weeks until one day a man said I'd charged him a penny too much. A second attempt produced the same total but I graciously said that he could keep the penny. However, despite an ever-lengthening queue, he insisted that we try again saying 'You must get it right, my dear'. At that point I disappeared under the counter in floods of tears and was sent by the kindly supervisor to get a cup of tea. I spent the next 12 Saturdays happily serving ice cream.'

Audrey Joyner

A superior range of Saturday girls

'When I reached the age of 15 and became eligible for a Saturday job, shop work appealed. But the headmistress of the girls' grammar school I attended did not like us having jobs: she thought that we had enough schoolwork to occupy us. Most shops in the area knew this but still asked her for references – Woolworth's was the only one which did not enquire. Consequently the Twickenham branch had a very superior range of Saturday girls! I was put to work on the sweet counter and I remember that after my first day I had a sleepless night, my head whirling as I tried to count up how much a handful of chocolate should be when all the pieces were priced variously at 1d, 1½d, 2½d, and so on. Everything had to be worked out in your head, including the giving of change, as there were no automatic tills.

At the end of the sweet counter was a cross-counter selling cake, which was cut to order. This was the preserve of an older, full-time member of staff who liked to guard it very jealously. I remember the sense of pride when she decided that I was a suitable person to train to take over from her at tea breaks and lunchtimes.

Towards the end of my time there they introduced the first automatic tills on the self-service grocery section. Sometimes I was put there, although I don't remember enjoying it very much as you didn't get the opportunity to chat to the customers, and you were marooned in one place, away from other staff.

We had a management team of three: the manager, his deputy and a floorwalker, who was considered to be very 'dishy' by us young girls. Under them was a staff supervisor and a number of section supervisors. As I recall, all the senior managers were men, while the supervisors were women.

One thing I do acknowledge as a result of those three years is that my knowledge of the hit parade was never as extensive again.

All day long the current hits were playing – it's lucky that I was a fan of the Mersey Sound!

Being in Twickenham meant that rugby home internationals brought a surge of customers stocking up with sweets as they made their way to the ground; then there would be a lull until after the match.

When I began work in 1962 I was paid 15 shillings for the day. I think it had risen to one pound by the time I left. If I worked for a whole week, I took home seven pounds, which seemed riches indeed. We were paid in cash at the end of each Saturday. We had to go up to the staff supervisor's office, where she gave us our little brown envelopes, from which was deducted any money we had spent on drinks or food in the staff canteen. There was always the opportunity of holiday work and some overtime.

One other thing I remember was Sir Winston Churchill's funeral, which happened in January 1965. I was working on a Saturday and the whole country shut down for three hours. Our store provided a television in the staff room so that we could watch if we wished.

It was a really happy time for me: I had some school friends working with me, but the regular staff were great fun too. We were all treated well, the staff supervisor making sure that we all had our statutory breaks – morning, lunch and afternoon – and there were regular customers to look forward to. I only gave up a couple of months before my A-levels began in order to do some more revision.'

Carol Anelay

Café romance

'I was employed in Woolies and one Saturday I was asked if I would mind being a waitress for the day due to staff shortages. Two young men were sitting at a table and one of them, whose name was Walter, was trying to chat me up. The other young man asked me if I would like to go to the pictures. His name was Ken and we have been together for 66 years.'

Connie Inman

An expert on everything

'I was a Saturday girl and school holiday relief in 1953 at the Chapel Street branch of Woolworth's at the Angel, Islington. In those days every girl wanted a Saturday job. I lived about four miles away but could not get a vacancy any nearer home. I earned 10 shillings a day less 3d for my National Insurance Stamp and, of course, I had to pay my own bus fare.

The store was extremely busy and Saturday girls were moved to any counter where extra staff were needed – sometimes to the tea bar or stock room. Woolies sold almost everything and that meant you had to be an expert on anything from food and drapery, to nuts and bolts. The beauty of it, which would be appreciated now in this time of recession, was that you could buy two screws, a quarter-yard of ribbon or half a pound of broken biscuits – any amount you wanted without having to buy a whole bagful. Each counter was divided into small sections about nine or 12 inches square and the walls all around the store were lined with polished wood with glass mirror panels.'

Maureen Forsyth

Tea with Mrs Thatcher

'In 1987 I was a winner in the Woolworth's Leadership scheme. This scheme was designed to introduce the subject of leadership and personal development into the school curriculum. Woolworth's contacted about 7,000 schools and youth groups nationwide and there was a competition to find young people aged between 14 and 17 who displayed outstanding leadership qualities. I was 15 years old and a pupil at Eastbourne Comprehensive School in Darlington when I learnt that I was one of 24 winners across the country.

Our prize was an amazing two days in London which included a visit to the Oval, and to Henley College and afternoon tea with the Prime Minister, Mrs Thatcher. At Woolworth House I had lunch and met all the other winners, before we began the afternoon's activities at Henley Management College where we even did abseiling from a huge tower made of scaffolding.

The following morning we were presented with our certificates

Annalisa Hopkins receiving her Woolworth's Leadership certificate from
TV personalities Keith Chegwin and Maggie Philbin in 1987

by TV personalities Keith Chegwin and Maggie Philbin who
made very amusing speeches. Over lunch at the Oval Cricket
Ground we met Lady Howe, who has done an awful lot of work
for equal rights; Chris Bonnington the famous climber, and Peter
Powell, the Radio 1 disc jockey, who spent the time having his
photo taken with all the girls! then it was off to meet the Prime
Minister herself.

As we neared the barriers to Downing Street, we all started to
panic: we climbed down from the coach, with the TV cameras
rolling and the press photographers snapping away. At last we entered
No.10 where we were ushered into a room, there was a deadly hush
as a little lady entered the room and we were face to face with the

Picture: Annalisa Hopkins

Winners of the Woolworth Leadership Programme meet the Prime Minister, Margaret Thatcher, at 10 Downing Street. Annalisa Hopkins is shown on the left in the front row

Prime Minister. A maid brought tea for us all and we stood together chatting with Mrs Thatcher. Everything was so relaxed.

I became a Saturday girl at our local store; my mother joined me there as a member of the office staff and later on the shop floor for over 20 years.'

Annalisa Hopkins

Dressing the windows

'I am 70 years old but still have clear memories of working on the counters and the shop-floor of the Muswell Hill store when I was 15 or 16. I was asked to train as a window dresser: they had big bay windows then. I'm still working in retail now.'

Pauline Seers

Snowstorms and ping-pong balls

'When I was 14 I became a Saturday morning assistant in Woolworth's in Terminus Road, Eastbourne. Going for an interview with the manager was quite simple and involved doing a few sums. I think he was more interested in which school you went to.

I was paid 3s 3d an hour, which was better than the Co-op at 2s 6d an hour, but not as good as Marks and Spencer. I was put on the toy counter and loved it. A school friend was on the haberdashery just opposite. My counter had a mass of small sections divided by pieces of glass and kept in place by metal clips. Each compartment would have a few bags of marbles, balloons, cars, cowboys, mouth organs, snowstorms or ping-pong balls. As soon as you had sold something, you were supposed to find some more under the counter and fill up the section.

Sometimes the refill box ran out or a customer wanted a few dozen balloons, then you had to go upstairs to the stock room to fetch some more down. What an Aladdin's cave it was up there! Some stock was seasonal, such as tennis balls, skipping ropes, swim-rings and spades. But there seemed to be stock that never came down whatever the season.

Picture: author's collection

A huge colour-range of Sylko sewing threads, all available at 6d per reel, in this display dating from the late 1950s

Later, I was allowed to work on Friday evenings and bank holidays. I got on well with the woman who ran the counter: she used to make comparisons between morn-ing and afternoon girls and keep us all on our toes. I loved the times when I was by myself running the counter and keeping everything shipshape.

Another girl I met there was Pauline, whose mother also worked in Woolworth's. One year I persuaded her to send a Valentine card to a boy I knew called John. I also persuaded him to send one with a date in it to Pauline. Although neither knew each other, I told them both that they would really like each other. So they met, did like each other and eventually got married with myself as a bridesmaid.'

Helen Meyrick

Artistic display

'When I was 15, I spent Saturday mornings and school holidays working in the Luton branch, on the hardware counter selling such items as carbolic soap and toilet rolls. The counter was wooden with high sides and a gap for the assistant to enter. The floor surrounding the counter was made of wooden boards which were highly polished. I had my own cash till and remember arranging the toilet rolls into a pretty pattern and displaying all the other cleaning materials in a similar way. The manager asked if I was interested in becoming a supervisor, but I told him I wanted to work in administration. I stayed on at High School until I was 16 then joined the council as a junior clerk at Luton Town Hall.'

Joyce Young

'You look clean, dear'

'I remember with fond affection the two years (1965-1967) when I spent as a Saturday girl at Woolworth's in Market Harborough before starting my training to become a qualified nurse. I worked alongside a full-time worker nicknamed 'Gran' and another Saturday girl called Jackie who also became a nurse. I originally started on the counter selling seeds and shallots, but was told that as I looked 'clean' I would be moved to the biscuit counter.

We were paid 10 shillings for a Saturday, duly handed to us in a brown envelope at the end of the day by the store manager. We received two envelopes at Christmas. We wore a uniform of a white wrap-around overall and were expected to launder it ourselves. Lunch was taken in shifts in the canteen upstairs and was a wholesome dish produced by the resident cook at a very reasonable price. When I started my nurse training I often popped into the store to see 'Gran', a friendship which lasted right up until she died. I often relate my memories of Woolworth's to my children and grandchildren.'

Lynda Buckingham

Worldly-wise

'While I was a 17-year-old at Sutton Coldfield College, I went to work at Woolworth's on the Parade in the town centre to earn some pocket money. This was in 1969 and as a Saturday girl, I got the princely sum of £5 for a day's work. The hours were 8am to 6pm.

My uniform was a cheap yellow nylon overall which crossed at the front and tied at the back. My first day was on the sweet counter which was situated at the front of the store by the big double doors. There was a large red weighing machine by these doors and my colleagues and I entertained ourselves during quiet moments, watching people's embarrassed reactions as they entered the doors and promptly tripped over the machine. There were two of us on the sweet counter. The worst customers were the young children who came in and spent ages deliberating on which pick 'n' mix sweets to choose. They always seemed to do it when we were particularly busy. I remember occasionally ducking down behind the counter to pinch the odd sweet from the boxes, which were used to fill up the pick 'n' mix.

There was a huge room underneath the building where the stockroom boys worked. Occasionally I was sent down there to order boxes of sweets we had run out of, but I never liked going: it was a strange and gloomy place. That's until I fancied a stockroom boy, when I would take a fraction longer to order the sweets because we would steal a kiss behind the shelving. Very exciting!

There was a canteen at the very back of the store where we could go to have our 15-minute morning and afternoon breaks and our half-hour lunch break. We could order a proper meal but we had to pay for it. I never ordered a meal after watching our cook's cigarette ash drop into several meals as she served up the plates, cigarette incredibly dangling from her mouth while keeping up a constant tirade of chatter.

I eventually graduated to the bread and meat counter which was opposite the sweet counter in the corner of the store. There was a lot more to do on this counter and I missed eating the sweets. We had a slicer so we could slice the loaves of bread if the customer wanted. We also sold sandwich meat such as corned beef, which I had to slice. I worked with a girl called Pam, who was a few years older than myself, and who I was a little in awe of. I thought she was very glamorous and worldly-wise – and she had a boyfriend. Pam and I went on holiday together to the Isle of Wight for a week, my very first holiday away from home without mum and dad. More than 30 years on, Pam and I still keep in touch.'

Sue Cooke

My 'chocolate' personality

'Woolworth's in Taunton was a gorgeous old-fashioned store with a wooden frontage and curved glass windows: it had lovely dark wood counters, too tall for small children to peer over! All the goods, such as scarves, gloves and toiletries, were laid out on flat surfaces like huge tabletops, and everything was folded, lined up and displayed really neatly. In addition to the things 'modern-day' stores sold, we had fruit and veg, delicatessen, cut-to-measure rolls of Fablon, broken biscuits, pick 'n' mix sweets and misshapen chocolates.

As a Saturday girl, my favourite counter to work on was the pick 'n' mix as the stocks were kept under the shelf, and as we walked up and down the centre aisle of the displays we could duck down and help ourselves to the odd chocolate, under the pretence of re-stocking supplies. I think this may be where my 'chocolate' personality began.

At the tender age of 17, I also on occasion had do the cooking and serve lunch all by myself, to the staff. No food hygiene or health and safety certificates or risk assessments then. Just 'here's the stuff, get on with it'. Thank goodness they demanded nothing more adventurous than toast for elevenses, fish fingers, peas and mash for lunch, and Swiss roll or lemon curd sandwiches for afternoon tea.

The funniest, or possibly the most frustrating, thing I recall was the lift. The stockroom was upstairs, so to bring a trolley full of goods to the shop floor we had to use the lift – the sort that had a 'cage door' that had to be pulled across. It didn't automatically stop at floor level: you had to push a button to stop it. Whether it was in the right place was more by luck than judgement and, for me, it was usually two inches too high or too low. You didn't find this out until you tried to get the trolley in or out – then you had to close the door and try again. You could be in there for quite some time.

We also had to add up all the prices in our heads or on a piece of paper, as none of the tills added up automatically. I wonder how many younger people would be prepared to do that now or be able to work out how much change a customer was due, especially when they offered 'the odd change'?

My time at Woolies was great fun and a great introduction to the adult world of work. It paid for some new clothes, and a Saturday night out, wearing the same ridiculously painful platform shoes that had been crippling me all day while on my feet behind the sweet counter. Oh happy days. As a matter of fact, some of my classmates – a number of whom also worked at Woolies – had a get-together in 2009 to celebrate out 50th birthdays, so there was plenty of opportunity to reminisce about our Saturday jobs.'

Sue Porter

They saw me coming!

'When I became a Saturday girl at Woolworth's in Commercial Road, Portsmouth, around 1959, they put me on the plant counter because that particular counter wasn't manned. I soon found out why. It meant that I had to get in earlier in the morning to fetch the plants in from the yard and then, after the shop closed, I had to take them back out and water them. I imagine the full-time staff were very pleased to see young naïve girls like me.'

Bonnie Comlay

Different branches, different wages

'I went with my friend to apply for a Saturday job at the London Road, Portsmouth, store in 1966. She was a month older then me, so we waited until I was 15 and we could go together. We had to do a 30 minute test, which I seem to remember contained a lot of arithmetic. There were three stores in Portsmouth and each had a different rate of pay: Southsea was 17s 6d, Commercial Road was £1 2s 6d and London Road was £1 a day. We had to pay 3d for our Insurance Stamp out of that. When I left school I went full time for three weeks as I could not start my job in the bank until after my 16th birthday. I enjoyed my year in Woolworth's and still see a couple of people I worked with.'

Rita Waight

Greasy pots and pans

'In 1946 I had just turned 14 years of age and my first job was at Woolworth's in Preston. During the war my twin sister and I didn't get much education, and as a result could not read properly. I worked on the jewellery and record counters situated on the far wall on the left: our first task in the morning was to wash down all this part of the store. Then we had to dust down all the counters that we worked on, and after lunch we had to go in the tea-bar and wash up all the customers' pots in the same greasy water. It was awful. We also couldn't go into work if our overall pockets were not sewn up. They were very strict with the young ones. We even had to go shopping for the bosses, which I didn't mind because I thought the time went quicker.

At the top of the store there was an office like a stage and the manager used to stand up there and have a good look around to see if everybody was working. If you were just standing still he would shout at the top of his voice and tell you off, even when the store was open with customers all around.

The only thing I liked about Woolworth's was when boxes of chocolates came in and the staff got first choice, the offer being two small bars each – that happened about every two months. We also used to get Ponds Cold Cream for our mum and she was thrilled to bits.'

Betty Hogg

One day's work = one 7-inch single

'In 1972 when I was 14, a few of us used to go into Woolworth's at Fishergate, Preston, and work for an hour stacking shelves, from 4.30pm until 5.30pm. For this we used to be paid just over £4 per week, which meant either a trip to the cinema or a 7-inch record from Brady's music shop.

When I became old enough I became a Saturday girl. Two of the full-timers there were sisters with the surname Mistry. One went to work for Sainsburys in Preston but I believe the other worked at Woolworth's until quite recently. She used to recognise me when I went in to shop, even though I am now a 50-year-old and my youngest daughter is now the age I was when I started working after school.'

Susan Stainton

Not good enough for her 'gels'

'I was on the cosmetics counter at Woolworth's in Fishergate, Preston, as a Saturday girl in 1959 and 1960, and I loved earning some money of my own to spend on clothes, make-up and going to the local dances on Saturday nights. At the end of the day when the store had closed and cashing up had been done, covers had to be put over the counters. A bell rang and the Saturday girls had to queue up and be handed their pay. I think I earned 11s 6d for a day's work.

Somehow the headmistress of my school, a new and rather posh establishment called Penwortham Girls Grammar School, got to know about my job and I was asked to go to her room. She explained that she didn't like her 'gels' having weekend jobs as she felt it would interfere with our studies (as though we would have spent all day Saturday studying). Other girls worked in places like British Home Stores or Marks and Spencer, but they didn't get called in to see her. I think she thought Woolies was not quite good enough for her pupils. I loved it and felt really grown up working with full-time staff, especially when they talked about their boyfriends, they being older than me.'

Sheila Marsh

You can't eat nails and screws

'I always wanted to work on the sweet counter, I think because I was deprived of sweets during the war, but when I started at Woolworth's in Stockton on Tees in 1957 as a Saturday girl, they put me on the counter that sold nails and screws. I did move on to fancy goods at one time and continued to work at Woolworth's until leaving college at about 16 years of age. I used to work full-time in the school holidays: I made many friends and have many happy memories.'

Sandra Capes

Just like *Open All Hours*

'My wages as a Saturday girl in 1953 at Woolworth's in Stockton-on-Tees in County Durham were 6 shillings an hour, less 6d for insurance. I worked on the electrical counter testing light bulbs, measuring flex and advising on lamp shades. I had to add up all the purchases in my head, punch the amount into the till (I loved that till, it was like Arkwright's in the TV show *Open All Hours*) and work out the change. Our headmistress was not keen on her grammar school girls working in Woolworth's, but when I left at 16 she did comment on my initiative.

I went on to do office work but have very fond memories of my particular branch of Woolies with its individual counters and wooden floors. It closed in the 1970s but opened up again across the high street in a shopping precinct, where it remained until the credit crunch closed all the Woolworth's stores.'

Barbara Ball

Coconut mushrooms and Pontefract cakes

'I worked on the sweet counter as a Saturday girl, and through my six-week summer holidays, at the Redcar store in the early 1960s. Customers would ask for a quarter of a particular sweet, such as coconut mushrooms. We weighed them and put them in a white paper bag and then, if they wanted more of another type of sweet such as Pontefract cakes, chocolate drops, nougat, or jelly babies, we weighed them too and we had to add up all the purchases in our head. We had to have good mental arithmetic skills. We also had to keep the counter well-stocked, nipping off to the stockroom during quieter periods to fetch more stock.

We had to clock in and out, and put on a wrap-around overall, usually stiff with starch, and a cap to keep our hair away from the sweets. Miss Bean, who I think was the manager, used to keep a close eye on everyone from her office on the shop floor. Redcar race days were particularly busy, with coaches arriving bringing the men to the races, and the women and children to the town and the beach. The days usually passed very quickly as it was always hectic. At the end of the day we had to sweep up behind the counter, fill up the sweets and then place large white sheets over everything. I recall the pay was 15 shillings a day. My sister and many of my friends also worked as Saturday girls and we were all very sad to see the store close as we have many memories of those years.'

Kathleen Thompson

A balaclava for a budgie

'When I was 14 my mother, who worked in the office at Woolworth's in Yeovil, arranged interviews for myself and a school friend Annie for Saturday jobs. At that time, in 1961, we were 14 so were only allowed to work a four-hour day. We took a maths test and started work a week later.

At that time staff working on the counters wore turquoise overalls and, being so young and small, the ones I was given were big and baggy. Supervisors wore dark blue. I was first put on the jewellery counter but after a while I worked on most of the counters including toiletries and household.

Life is so much easier now with scanning tills that total the sale and tell the assistant what change to give. In those days we learnt the prices of items and had to be able to total, press the right keys on the tills and give the correct change. And dealing in pounds, shillings and pence was much more difficult.

In the centre of the store, we would stand in the middle of the wooden counters and serve on all four sides. I remember the cosmetics, separated by glass, with clip-on price tags.

Then there was the biscuit counter with loose biscuits and one tub containing broken biscuits, all of which had to be weighed. On the gardening counter, we had to dig out plants from large trays and wrap them in newspaper. Lampshades were displayed above the counters and we had to fetch them for customers from the stockroom upstairs. I also remember Embassy records (I still have two in my collection) and always enjoyed being put on the fancy goods counter so that I got to choose which records to put on. While on the household/pet counter, I can remember being asked for a 'tin of chequered paint' and a 'balaclava for a budgie'.

At the age of 14 the grand total of my earnings for four hours' work was six shillings: when I turned 15, I was able to work full time and had a pay increase. It was a great thrill at Christmas and New Year to receive a bonus of an extra week's pay: another six shillings, and later fifteen shillings and then a pound.

Above the main floor of the store were the stockroom, locker room, cloakrooms and a staff canteen, where you could buy a delicious lunch. Members of staff were friendly and helpful and I can still recall the names of many of them. Over the time I worked

Picture: Evelyn Baines

Celebration for Redcar staff after winning the 1956 October Shield for 'best store' of the year

there I made some special friends. A few years ago, five of us started to meet up again for lunch in Exeter. My school friend Annie, office worker Janet and I now all live in Devon. Gillie, who also worked in the office, comes from her home in Kent to stay with me for a few days and Ann from the stockroom comes down from Yeovil. We have all remained friends for over 45 years.'

Marilyn Fursey

Party prize

'I worked at the old Woolworth's in Redcar, first as a Saturday girl and then full time for 18 years on leaving school. My sister Evelyn Baines also worked at the store and in 1956 we won the 'best store' shield: as a reward, we were all invited to a staff party.'

Barbara Sill

'Pops' led our Woolies family

At Woolworth's in Gosport, Hampshire, we called our manager 'pops' as he was like a father to all his staff. I was 15 years old and it was my first experience of working: I loved putting on my pink overall and serving people. We had a tea break in the morning and afternoon, and you paid a small amount for your dinner. I was entitled to a discount, so that year all my Christmas presents and cards were bought in Woolies. I was becoming independent now.

Picture: Evelyn Baines

Picture: Barbara Sill

Junior staff at the Redcar store in the early 1950s

Redcar staff showing off the October Shield

I served on the haberdashery counter and fruit counter, but my regular counter sold a mixture of seeds, flower bulbs, plants, shoe insoles, shoe cleaning products, laces, glue and stick-on soles for doing your own repairs. It also sold dog and cat food.

I started work at 9am, and my first task was to polish the wooden counters and fill up with stock underneath so that we didn't run out during the day. We had to add up purchases in our head or use a piece of paper if there were lots of items. One day I was asked to help the lady in the upstairs stockroom tidying the crockery, tea/dinner sets and glasses. I worked there during one of my Christmas holidays and the extra money enabled me to buy some math sets for my schoolwork.'

Linda Smart

Chatting with the stars

'The store at Aston Cross, Birmingham, was next to the ATV studios, so all the stars of *Crossroads* used to come in when I was a Saturday girl there in 1963. Noele Gordon, who played Meg Richardson in the show, was lovely: she used to talk to all of us. My pay was 16s 11d for a Saturday, but when I worked the school holidays I got a whole £5. It's amazing what I bought out of the Saturday money: stockings for 2s 11d, chocolate for my mom, and even a present for the dog. Definitely the good old days. Part of my job was going to the storeroom, which was up in the Gods, and everybody said there was a ghost up there. I was terrified.

On my counter we sold cleaning goods and one day I broke a bottle of ammonia. All day my eyes were watering and the customers thought I was crying and kept saying 'keep the change' as they thought I was hard up.

My gran used to come in and stand by the counter telling every customer I was her granddaughter: the supervisor had to tell her to go home. It was good that we could add up in those days, not like with these fancy tills that add up and work out the change for you.

My biggest regret in life is that I didn't stay there but my dad wanted me to get a job in an office. He worked at Ansells Brewery, as all my family did, so I was given a job there.'

Sandra Reynolds

Look out – here comes Mr Hare

'The manager at the Cardigan branch, where I was a Saturday girl from 1967-69, was called Mr Hare. He was quite strict and used to walk around the store all day. We would hear his shoes make a rhythmic tap-tap around the corner on the old-fashioned floorboards and knew he was near.

Before I was taken on I had to take an arithmetic test and found this very daunting, as it was my least favourite subject at school. But I passed and was given a green uniform. My first counter was the lightbulbs: there was a gadget to test each bulb and it took me a while to master this.

All the staff took their lunch in the canteen on the top floor and were given three lunchtimes; 11.30am – 12.30pm, 12.30 – 1.30 or 1.30 – 2.30. The first one was never popular because the afternoon seemed to go on for ever: the 1.30 lunch was the one everybody wanted, but only the permanent staff had this time slot.

We sold ladies fashions in those days and I had my eye on a bright pink quilted dressing gown ready for when I was going to Teacher Training College in Cardiff. I was able to put it away and pay for it in weekly instalments out of my Saturday wages – this took quite a long time.

The competition by the Saturday girls to be given work in the summer holidays was fierce and the only fair way was to be given one week each. My pay for Monday to Saturday was £5 but after paying tax and stamp (the National Insurance of today) I was left with a meagre amount. At least I have a history of payments from age 16 and will therefore qualify for a full state pension when the time comes!'

Ethne Biggs

Different rooms

'The store in Cardigan had several different rooms, each with the old-fashioned wooden floor, and each section had its own counter and cash till. I worked there as a Saturday girl in 1967-68 and thoroughly enjoyed it. I often worked on the broken biscuit counter.'

Ulia Davies

'I'm next, Miss!'

'On my counter at the Kingswood store in Bristol we sold a mixture of items, and there was a large cash register which had a bell that sounded as the drawer opened and closed. The counter was very long and, at one end, cups, saucers and plates were displayed. Each crockery item had to be wrapped in newspaper before being placed in a brown paper bag. Next came the assortments of daps (plimsolls), plastic sandals, leather soles taps for toes and heels of shoes (to prolong the life of the footwear), and various colours and length of shoe and bootlaces. Displayed next to this were electrical items such as light bulbs which had to be tested on a wooden block with a brass switch. Fuses and batteries had to be tested too, by placing them on a contraption that would buzz if successful. We also had reels of electrical wire of different colours and cores with a yard measure beneath to measure off the length requested by the customer. On this section above our heads hung the lampshades of various colours and shapes – even the odd plastic mock-chandelier.

There was no form of queuing: just a mass of people standing in front of the long counter all holding out their various items, shouting that they were the next to be served. It was hard work but very enjoyable. I was there as a Saturday girl for two years, starting in 1961 when I was 14. All these years down the line I am still in the retail business, working in a large Tesco on the checkouts, I love my job and relish the customer contact.'

Gloria Hiscox

It seemed like a fortune

'The West Street shop in Havant, Hampshire, was a long shop with wooden floors. Two long counters ran down each side, with three island counters down the middle. The sales staff and tills were in the middle of the islands. Miss Dorothy Grant was the supervisor and I believe she had been there all of her working life. I remember being put on the biscuit counter selling broken biscuits, and on the gardening counter selling loose potting-compost. I was 14 when I worked there, from November 1960 to June 1962. The wages were 10s 6d per Saturday – a fortune to me in those days.

Later, when I received the staff discount. I used to buy a few groceries each week to help my parents' food bill.'

Maureen Cawte

Lucky break

'I worked as a Saturday girl in the Soho Road, Handsworth, Birmingham store during 1959. I really loved working there: it was a friendly place and I was lucky enough to be put on the counter selling make up and toiletries. This was considered to be the best counter. No-one liked to be on biscuits, as in those days they were sold loose and had to be weighed. Also disliked was the electrical counter, because every light bulb sold had to be tested.

The pay from 9am until 6pm was 16 shillings. We had 30 minutes for lunch and could buy a freshly cooked meal in the canteen for 1s 10d. I was aged 15 at the time and only left when I had to study for GCSE exams in summer 1960.'

Anne Payne

Let there be light!

'I started as a Saturday girl in the same store as my mother, Phyl Darlington, at Goring. It was a small self-service store with only three aisles and two checkouts. The only counter with staff was the sweet counter. Each of the Saturday girls was allocated a department to 'fill up': this meant writing a list of what stock was needed. We used wire baskets to get the stock unless it was something bulky. I did the electrical counter most of the time when I started and then progressed to sweets and the checkout. One of the jobs on 'electrical' was checking that the light bulbs worked before customers bought them. You fitted the bulb into the socket and pressed the button. Hey presto! Many of them did not work, so it was obviously a good idea. In the stockroom the light bulbs were on the top of the shelving. There were very tall stepladders to reach the top but they were difficult to manoeuvre, so it was often easier to scale the racking shelf by shelf, with one foot either side of the aisle. Not at all ladylike. Having reached the top, the bulbs were removed from the box and, as you descended, you moved them down the shelves. If you only needed a few, the box was passed down to someone to take out what was needed before it was passed back. No one thought about health and safety.

On the sweet counter my first job was to switch on the light bulb under the roasted peanuts. This kept them warm, so first thing in the morning was not the best time to buy them. Filling them up was messy, as the bag was heavy and oily; you had to wait until the tray was empty and put in a full bag. All the sweets were weighed in quarters. I did it so long I could just take a handful of Devon Toffees (best-seller) and it would be a quarter. We had pick 'n' mix of higher quality sweets than today. Quality Street and Roses were included, so you could pick just your favourites.

Last thing at night one of us had to sweep the shop floor, sprinkling sawdust first. None of us liked doing this. When I worked on the checkout I had to take my own cash-drawer to the till. Should someone take over later, they would bring theirs and I would take mine to the office for checking. At the end of the day the last drawer was checked and no-one got their pay packet or left until it was done. I worked in the Goring store with my mother during school holidays, so we sometimes had lunch together. I spent most of my pay packet on shoes, but some went on makeup from Woolies.'

Jan Dineen

Private eye

'One particular day, when I was working as a Saturday girl in the Hemel Hempstead branch in the early 1980s, I thought I was going to be the hero of the store. I was following closely behind a suspicious-looking person in order to catch them red-handed when they eventually stole something. Unfortunately for me, it turned out I had been trailing the store detective!'

Kate Burridge

A little white lie

'Being a Saturday girl was something I couldn't wait to do, so in 1964 I lied about my age. I was only 14 at the time. I joined the shop in High Road, Wood Green, London: it had wooden counters, each with its own cash register. The very first customer

I served, I gave one shilling too much in change. It was nerve-racking at the beginning. My first wage packet contained 17s 6d and I spent every penny on my mum, including buying her an iced cake and a miniature rose bush. The bush survived in her front garden for 30 years. Woolies sold garden plants and I would get an extra 2s 6d for getting my hands dirty.'

Norma Spriggs

Too shy to mix

'At 15 years of age I was a shy Saturday girl working with my friend Kathy Bowdidge in the plimsoll department on the bottom floor of the store in Exeter High Street where we had to pair them up in sizes, put an elastic band around them and place them in the right display spot. Behind the huge display counter was a large old radiator, which − as we were too shy to eat in the staff canteen − is where we would eat our sandwiches. When we reached 16 we were allowed too work on a till: boy, did we think we were important! I remember the big brass stair rail (always highly polished), the wooden floors and different counters.'

Sandra Redwood

Service with compassion

'I worked all my adult life as a secretary until 1989, when I became a Saturday girl at Woolworth's in The Parade at Sutton Coldfield. I was there for over six years, running the customer service desk, then moving up to the office. I used to empty the tills during the day and take the money to the office for accounting. I became close friends with the office manageress, Rose, and when I reached my 50th birthday, Rose took me out for a drink. She walked up to this posh restaurant and I said 'we can't go in there', but eventually I agreed to go in. As I went up the stairs, *Happy Birthday* was being played, the lights went up and there was the complete staff of Woolworth's. It was one of the best nights of my life. I had for a long time loved the Royal Doulton figurines of the ladies in lovely dresses but as yet did not own one: that night I had my first lady as the staff had bought me one for my birthday.

I owe a lot to Woolworth's: even as a young girl, my fiancé and

I used to buy something every week from the store in the Old Bull Ring, for my bottom drawer. I will also be forever grateful to Woolworth's because of how they helped me when my lovely mother died. As I had lost my husband to cancer, my mother and I lived for each other and her loss left me completely broken. I was trying to sort out the best funeral I could for her. Both of us loved El Divo and I had bought her their version of *Mama*. I wanted this to be playing when she was brought into the church. However, I could not find the CD, just the empty case. I was devastated and it was only a few days till the funeral. I went to my Sutton Coldfield branch of Woolworth's and explained the situation. 'Don't worry madam, we will obtain it for you', they said. I duly left my name and address and left, not holding out much hope. Just 24 hours later, a representative of Woolworth's was at my front door with the recording. I challenge any company to beat that, it's what I can only call perfect service, with kindness and compassion.'

Shirley E Smith

Scraping off the mould – all part of the job

'I remember the camaraderie of the Saturday boys and girls at High Road, Wood Green, London, and the learning experience of earning £4.10 for a day's work. This was 1975. In fact I also learned that if you do a day's work, but forget to sign in, then there is no brown bag with £4.10 at the end of the day.

It's illegal now unless you are 18 or over, but I learned the skill of operating a mechanical food slicer and enjoyed slicing off a quarter of ham or corned beef for the customers. Our manager on the deli counter was feared but he was probably only in his 20s and still learning his own trade. If he told you to do something you did it even to the point of going up to the walk-in cold store and scraping the mould off the huge blocks of Cheddar cheese. We served out the paté in quarters from huge bowls which, if not claimed by the customer buying the last portion, were fair game for the staff. A career in Environmental Health beckoned, so those early days of experiencing life on the other side of the counter were invaluable.

As well as Saturdays, my summer holidays of 1975 were spent

working at Woolies. One day I was given the opportunity of being a floorwalker. What bliss! I could walk around the store with the brief of keeping shelves tidy and possibly looking out for shoplifters. I was my own boss. Well almost. It was an opportunity to talk with other workers who I had only seen from the safety of the deli counter.

Another enjoyable task was to work in the storerooms compacting the waste cardboard into bales and helping to move goods around the store. The staff canteen was a welcome refuge and offered a chance to rest and recuperate.

In January 1976 the dream was over – O-levels beckoned and I sadly said goodbye to Woolworth's. And Woolworth's also soon said farewell to its deli counter and stopped serving food. Now pick 'n' mix would be the only way to buy 'open' food.'

Derek Pearce

Only slightly singed

'My mum worked in Woolworth's in the Market Place, Leicester, when I was a child, and in the early 1950s there was a fire at the store. I don't think anyone was hurt, but the staff were given or allowed to buy the salvaged stock. My mum brought a small doll home for me – it had singed hair. I thought it was lovely and I still have it to this day. I am now 63.

When I was 18 and at college and needed a part-time job, Woolworth's was the obvious choice. Both my friend and I landed a Saturday job there. Our pay was 19s 11d and I was put on the shoe counter selling shoes, polish, laces and so on. It was a rude awakening into the working world for me; I wasn't very confident and nor was I keen on all the rules and regulations. I was training to be a shorthand typist at the time. Being one of five children, we were all encouraged to work for what we wanted, and there was no slacking in our house. I have to admit that, most weeks, there wasn't a lot left of my 19s 11d. After all, it was my first real wages.

I enjoyed being sent to the warehouse for extra stock. I usually got told off for being too long down there! And of course the best bit was leaving at night with wages in hand (what was left of them after lunchtime spending). My friend and I loved looking around the market for bargains. There was one memorable occasion when both of us had spent almost every penny and realised we hadn't got enough bus fare to get home. Thankfully my friend was able to reverse the charge in the phone box and ring her uncle, who kindly came to get us. We didn't do that again.'

Pat Rowley

Eye-opener for 'posh girls'

'I look back very fondly at the memories and experiences I had as a Saturday girl at Woolworth's on The Parade, Sutton Coldfield. I started in 1967 as a 15-year-old and worked there for three years, sometimes through the holidays too. I went to Sutton Coldfield Grammar School for girls and at Woolworth's I started on 17 shillings and sixpence a week for a Saturday. It was my chance for some independence. The store was housed in an old Victorian building, and there were old-style counters with assistants behind most of them, offering old-fashioned, personal service. I worked on the counter that sold bread, biscuits cooked meats, and cheese.

There was a marked difference between the Saturday girls and the full-time staff. We were regarded as 'quite posh' because we attended the Grammar School. It was my first experience of getting to know really great working-class people at a personal level. I liked pretty much everyone who worked there and remember being shocked and horrified when people confided details about their personal lives – one of the girls had a violent boyfriend and came in with black eyes on a fairly regular basis. Another woman suffered from her husband's mental cruelty and there were staff who had no money left at all by mid-month. One of the girls I made friends with had a very possessive, frightening stepfather who did not want her to have any boyfriends. I used to keep her love letters for her until she plucked up the courage to run away and marry her man – she was 24. Their stories started to open up my narrow and somewhat cushioned world, which I have been steadfastly opening further ever since.

Saturday was the busiest day of the week in Woolworth's then, and the bread counter on a Saturday morning, the busiest of all. I got to know my regular customers. My favourite was a little old man of 87, who used to come in for his 'Snowball' loaf every week. One week, not long after I started, we had already sold out of Snowballs when he came in, so I used to keep one for him each week after that. He seemed unhappy, and as I got to know him, he told me that he had recently lost his beloved wife of many years and was very lonely. I started to visit him after work, and used to bake a chocolate cake to take to his house. This was actually no mean feat, because I lived seven miles away from Sutton Coldfield in Castle Bromwich and the bus service was terrible. When I went to see my old gentleman, it meant I missed my only straight bus home and then had to catch three different buses which took me around an hour and a half.

I visited him regularly for over a year, until it became apparent that each time I visited, there was yet another little old lady there befriending him, and they all gave me fairly unfriendly looks! I laughed, and told him he didn't need me anymore, but we remained friends and he still came in for his loaf each week.

The managers in Woolworth's were quite strict, but on the whole very pleasant. They did praise you if you did something right. This was wonderful for me because some of the teachers at my school were harridans and gave only criticism. I was really frightened of some of them, especially the Religious Instruction teacher who used to come round and hit us at the slightest provocation. Praise at Woolworth's allowed me to think perhaps I wasn't quite the useless person that my school gave me the impression I must be, and was the beginning of a budding confidence.

The bread counter was right by the front of the store and so I was often called upon to watch out for thieves. One notorious thief was an old lady who wore a tacky-looking long raincoat, with numerous pockets inside it to conceal everything she took. One day after watching her stealing sweets and household items, the store manager and I followed her out of the store and down the road, where her colleague picked her up and whisked her away in her getaway Jaguar.

I met and worked with a great bunch of genuine, interesting colleagues in Woolworth's one of whom, Sue – another student Saturday girl – I am still privileged to call my friend today, 39 years later.'

Pam Reeve

THE SHOPPING EXPERIENCE

Mr and Mrs Woolies

'As a child in the late 40s and early 50s, a trip to Woolies was the most magical experience for all the bairns and myself in the small fishing village of Portessie in the North East of Scotland. The nearest Woolies town was Elgin and the journey there took us nearly two hours by bus. No-one started school without a visit to Woolies and when we reached 13 years of age, we would go there by ourselves – a great achievement. We bought our pencil cases, books, transfers and everything that was magical. Nowhere on earth could one purchase such exciting goods. At school we would discuss and compare our purchases. When we staged our school musicals, a trip to Woolies for the appropriate jewellery was a must and each one of us tried to outdo the other in the fashion stakes. Woolies had the answer.

When mothers usually advised us about the impending visit to Elgin, we had sleepless nights just thinking about it: we saved our pocket money to buy our goodies, and thought we were in heaven. The store had that mystical aroma which I can smell to this day and the staff were absolutely lovely, with time to chat to the adults and be patient with the children. It was a real family store.

We also got a visit from Mr and Mrs Woolies (as we named them), who appeared twice yearly with their red motorbike, sidecar and trailer. We would run home from school to see the Woolies: their presence caused the greatest excitement in the whole village. The couple were always well-dressed in their sheepskin coats and fur boots, and as children we were always so

Picture: Helen Main, courtesy of Catherine Adams

One big family: staff at the Elgin store in 1964. Left to right top row: Moira Watson, Meg McCook, Cathy Archibald, Emily Cameron, Doreen Danks and Mrs Scott; (bottom row): Diane Lang, Loretta Parsons, Jean McMurran, Ina Clark, Mary Cameron, Ilene Gordon and Helen Russell

impressed they knew our names and our families, which to us was so important.

We would purchase hair clips, jewellery and all sorts of things, and the adults would stand round the cart chatting and buying various goodies. Happy memories that will remain with me forever.'

Adeline Reid

What a temptation!

'There was a Woolworth's store on the main road opposite Lewisham Hippodrome. Everything was on ration at the time during the war, and my mum sent me round to Woolies for some biscuits. When I got to the biscuit counter, what a sight met my eyes! So many sorts, including chocolate and cream ones. But I just had to get a quarter-pound or thereabouts. Of course, I got the chocolate ones, paid the girl and left. The only snag was, by the time I had got home I had eaten one....or rather more than one. I got told off when I arrived home, as chocolate biscuits used up more ration coupons. I was made to take them back. The girl knew that one or two were missing but I just got away with it.'

Alan Kerry

Hair like an ice-cream cone

'Although never a particular fan of Woolworth's, I remember the glass boxes of broken biscuits in the late 1950s and early 1960s when I was a child. I loved these, especially the lemon-filled ones.

My main memory is of Portsmouth's Commercial Road branch: when I was a student in 1973 I bought Miner's perfume there for 30p or so for a tiny bottle (Mandarin was my favourite). The woman on the perfume and make-up counter was amazing: she wore inches of make-up and turquoise eye shadow. Her hair was dyed orange and styled in a huge, tall ice-cream cone shape on top of her head. I hope other people remember her, as she was something to see.'

Jacky Percival

Lead soldiers for a penny

'My fading memories of Woolies are of the store at Soho Road, in Handsworth, Birmingham in the 1930s when I was a schoolboy. It had an alternative name: 'The 3d and 6d Stores' and no item was priced above 6d. Lead soldiers were a penny upwards, Dinky Toys 6d, packets of stamps, such as the France Vimy Ridge pair, were a maximum of 6d. No doubt I spent some of my 6d a week pocket money there.'

W Philpott

Bottom drawer

'I bought numerous kitchen utensils for my bottom drawer from Woolworth's in Birmingham when I became engaged. I purchased one item every few weeks. These included mixing bowls, a teapot and a frying pan which I still use today more than 70 years later. I got them all for the grand sum of sixpence each: it was a lot of money out of my ten shillings weekly wage, having only 1s 6d pocket money each week.'

Olive Wiggett

A view of the moat

'Castle Street in Bristol was virtually destroyed by German bombers in 1940. This was a beautiful old street on part of the site of Bristol Castle. About halfway up Castle Street stood Woolworth's large shop, on the corner of Steep Lane running down to the harbour. Just inside the main entrance there was a wide stairway leading down to the basement which interested me greatly, because down below was the toy department.

My earliest memory must date from about 1932-33 when I would have been aged three. My mother took me into the ladies toilet and at some stage she picked me up held me up to the window. From there you could see the old moat of the castle. Since the wartime destruction, the moat is much more easily seen.

In the toy department, my older brother was very anxious for mum to buy him a Diablo, which consisted of two sticks to hold, with a string between them and an odd-shaped 'bobbin' which you could start spinning from stick to stick, performing all sorts of tricks, and making it jump and twist about.'

David Rees

Cowboy suits were best

'I remember the toy department in the Borehamwood store in 1960 or 1961: there were loads of Ladybird books on every subject you can imagine, big displays of Matchbox models, and toy guns that were made of steel and fired caps. The caps came in small, round cardboard boxes and cost 1d. I remember that cowboy suits always outsold Indian suits and bows and arrows. Spud guns were also popular at this time, as were kites, jacks, fivestones and plasticine. I think this is also the department where they sold puncture repair kits and inner tubes for bikes.'

Jean Croft

Chocolate liqueurs for 19p

'In the 1960s and 70s when I was growing up, Woolworth's was always the shop you made for on the high street. I remember the noisy, polished wooden floors and solid counters full of wire baskets of pick 'n' mix or Dinky Cars, the different mix of smells

– sweets, cheese, garden products and those black plimsolls we all used to wear for PE at school.

In Woolworth's you could spend your pocket money on Christmas gifts like bath salts, chocolate liqueurs for 19p, tins of salted peanuts, Cuthberts seeds and the Winfield brand.

On holiday or a day out, you always popped into Woolies to see if you could find a different pick 'n' mix or mum could find that plate to match those cups. Then there were Admiral swim shorts, buckets and spades, fizzy pop and cheap sunglasses for the beach. Chasing around in the

Picture: author's collection

car with dad to find that extra tin of Cover Plus paint in the same colour from another branch, and buying my first single and LP. And those big white tills, where sales staff had to enter a three-digit code for each item, were so slow printing the receipt you would be halfway down the street before it had finished! I remember having pie, chips, beans and a Coca Cola in the café, decorated in orange and lemon, with about 90 percent of the customers smoking cigarettes.

During the Winter of Discontent in 1979, Woolworth's was almost the only shop open, working by the light of candles and hurricane lamps, with the sales staff wearing several cardigans to try and keep warm.

The major changes occurred in the early 80s, with the removal of food retailing and the revamp of stores to introduce mockwooden floors, pale blue walls and the gold and red Woolworth's sign on a white background.'

Tim Godfrey

Building my farm set

'We had a lovely Woolies in Guernsey, Channel Islands, when I was young. It was a magical moment when you entered the store – the counters were full of toys and there was an assistant behind the counter to help you. Everything was 3d or 6d and I remember making up a farm set, taking my 3d to select the animals and farm buildings until it was complete several weeks later.'

Molly Gibson

Hard to choose

'My first memories of Redcar Woolworth's date from 1953 when I was seven years old and mother would take me and my sister Dorothy to buy something with our pocket money. We often chose a cut-out doll, which was dressed with paper clothes. The clothes had tabs on them to fasten onto the doll, and were cut or pressed out. We bought the doll one week and an outfit the next. We also bought colouring books and crayons. We always found it very difficult to make a choice and used to spend a long time choosing. Mam used to say 'if you don't make your minds up soon, I will leave you here'.'

Kathleen Thompson

Picture: author's collection

Don't despair if your carpets tear Just use our *Tapes* for quick repair

There are three types of tapes available in Woolworth stores, in a wide variety of widths and colours, none of which need sewing.
Iron-on Tapes in two thicknesses. Lightweight – plain finish, heavyweight – herringbone finish. Application : Place shiny side down and press with a moderately hot iron.
Bondfast Tape – No sewing or ironing required. Application : Peel off backing, place tape to carpet, press. All tapes are ideal for using on carpets, rugs, frayed materials, torn macs, etc.

It's well worth shopping at
WOOLWORTH

I still have the 'china lady'

'What a delight Woolworth's was in the 1930s! My first memory is my dad carrying me in the crowds to the Bull Ring store, Birmingham, on a Saturday. Then there was the store in New Street with its basement where my mam bought her china, art deco plates and a jug with a crocus painted on it.

The stores in the suburbs of Birmingham also have

memories. The newly built store in Lodge Road, Hockley, Birmingham known locally as the 'The Flat', where my mam bought me a china lady meant for putting on a tea-cosy or decorating a cake, I still have it to this day: I know it was sixpence and now is highly collectable as an antique.

Each district had its Woolworth's and if you went further afield in most towns you would see a Woolworth's store. I re-

A Dinky estate car from Derek Phillips' collection, bought for 2s 11d from Woolworth's in the 1950s. The range was extensive: a page from the catalogue can be seen in the colour section of this book

member being on holiday in Bournemouth before the Second World War and the store there having an upper floor; and Woolies in Teignmouth, Devon, where we bought presents for friends to take back home (ironically, years later, we were told the brooches we'd bought were made in the district we lived in – talk about 'Coals to Newcastle'!

The lady assistants always wore maroon-coloured dresses and worked two to a counter, one at each end. Every Christmas it was like a bun-fight to get cards – masses of them in different sections to suit all tastes and pockets. Whatever was required in the home, we always went to Woolworth's.'

Hazel Harwood

A big affection

'I well remember my visits in the 1930s to the various Woolworth's in Bristol. They were known as the 3d and 6d shops. Everything then was displayed on long counters and the shop assistants stood within the two counters to serve the customers. The shops were very special to people in those days, selling the things everyone needed: the name Woolworth's held a big affection for families in the 1930s and 40s.'

Olive Cooke

The Milky Way

'As a child I was a great fan of Harold Lloyd, the comedian, and I went with my parents to see all his films. They took me to the Carlton Cinema in London to see *The Milky Way*, in which Harold Lloyd plays a weedy milkman who accidentally becomes a champion boxer. This would have been about 1936. On the way back, we passed a Woolworth's and they had a big display in the window, promoting 'Milky Way Cocktails'. Right in the middle was a huge cardboard cut-out of Harold Lloyd in his milkman's uniform. Next day, I begged mum to take me into the store to try one. I remember not being able to decide between two flavours: one was Strawberry Flame and I think the other was called Silver Lady. The word 'cocktails' made them sound very glamorous, but I think they were really just milk-shakes.'

Annie Chaplin

Spalding bulbs

'Most of my childhood was spent in North Wiltshire, around Chippenham and Malmesbury. It was my parents who would take us to Woolworth's in Chippenham on a Saturday morning through most of the 1950s. They could shop and we could spend our pocket money. I thought the girls in their maroon uniforms seemed fantastically grown up. I can remember buying Spalding bulbs at about 6d and foreign stamps as I was a keen stamp-collector.'

Gordon Venables

Long life of mum's sixpenny dish

'My mother was married in 1934 and shortly afterwards she bought a large stoneware dish for 6d at the Crook branch in County Durham. It was used for baking bread every week, and the Christmas cake every year. When she died in 1990, we set bulbs in it every summer and put it in the garden. It is still going strong.'

Shirley Thompson

Cheap and cheerful

'When I was a child living in Eye, the highlight of a trip to Diss

A nine-inch plate from the Homemaker range of tableware designed by Enid Seeney in 1957 for Ridgway Potteries of Staffordshire and sold exclusively through Woolworth's. The design featured stylised illustrations of household items such as tables, lamps and chairs. Customers could buy one item at a time and build up a complete set. The Homemaker range is highly collectable today

was a visit to Woolworth's in Mere Street. In those days they had a counter at child height and assistants in maroon uniforms keeping an eye out for mini-shoplifters.

During the Second World War my gran bought her spectacles from Woolies and possibly her dentures. If they sold them, it was on the basis that one size fits all! While we were there she might buy me some hair slides, the round, brown plastic ones with moulded flowers on them, or those in the shape of pink or blue bows. I would wait while she sorted through the 'pearl' necklaces and the hankies.

After the war Woolworth's were one of the first shops to sell Kleeware plastic dolls' house furniture and little, bright, rubbery dolls to go into prams and highchairs. These are now collectors' items and fortunately I have kept some of mine.

When I was a bit older I would bike into Diss to the pictures and, of course, visit Woolies. I bought my first nail varnish from there (Longlex clear), and then lipstick (Tangee Natural). I was not allowed Californian Poppy perfume, but there was a deodorant called Snowflake. It was all part of a girl's growing up, as were my very first earrings, small screw-on pearls also from Woolies.

I remember the Homemaker brand of tableware made by Ridgway, a style icon of the 1950s. This was only sold in Woolworth's stores and is now revered by the antiques gurus. I bet there are still some of these in kitchen cupboards in Diss, as there are in mine.

Cheap and cheerful it may have been, but Woolies has been such a part of our lives that its loss is literally the end of civilisation as we know it. I was in our local Woolworth's in Caerphilly a few days before it closed, buying some copy paper. They had run out of big bags and I jokingly said I wanted the last plastic bag in existence. The cashier reached under the counter and produced one of their smallest sized carrier bags and said 'that is the last one in this store: in a few years time you can put it on eBay'. He also said that when I saw him selling the Big Issue, not to pass him by. I hope it hasn't come to that, as he was one of the most polite and obliging assistants in the local shops.'

Joy Matthews

Guilty, your honour!

'When I was a young child in the 1940s, my mother took me shopping in Exeter Woolworth's. I found a moth-ball and put it in my pocket. When we were about to leave, I realised I was doing the wrong thing, so I took it out of my pocket and left it on the counter.'

Margaret Campbell

Just like Jimmy Cagney

'Us wartime kids were deprived of any toys made of metal and even in 1946 the oh-so-slow return to a peacetime normal was still long and tedious. So when a kid in the next street in Gosport was seen with what looked like a real automatic -- just like the gats Jimmy Cagney used to plug anyone who got in his way in the movies -- I had to know where he got it.

'Look,' he said, 'it fires rolls of caps!' And he blazed away at me -- 'snap, snap snap!'

'They've gorrem in Woolworths,' he said. 'But they're half-a-crown, and tuppence a roll for the caps'.

I begged and pleaded and made all kinds of promises to borrow the money from mum – and rushed down the High Street, dead scared they'd be sold out. But Woollies (God bless 'em) had a dozen or more on the counter – neat, silver metal and perfect in every way; wonderful to the touch, a perfect fit in a boy's hand.

'Bang, bang, bang' – and for days I walked about in a cloud of gunsmoke and the acrid smell of gunpowder. Bliss.'

John Bull

Live wire

'I had a fascination with the electrical bits-and-pieces counter of the High Street, Gosport, branch when I was a young lad in the late 1950s. They had a yardstick to measure out the wires and flexes. I used to buy red and blue copper bell-wire by the yard (or maybe even foot) and bulb holders and switches. I'd wire them, in parallel or in series, to batteries for no particular purpose. At that time, each departmental counter was staffed by one or two girls enclosed within. I also remember wooden floors, Winfield own-brand paint, knitting needles and wool, Embassy records, Airfix kits with little pots of paint, Christmas paper chain kits and packets of crêpe paper, packets of stamps, stamp hinges for stamp collecting and hot roasted nuts.'

Picture: Steve Golding

Steve Golding wired up switches he bought at the Gosport store, just for fun

Steve Golding

Pride of place for ornaments

'When my mum was 13 years old in 1934, she contracted polio, then called Infantile Paralysis, and spent a year in hospital at Bath. It left her having to wear a calliper on her right leg for the rest of her life. After coming home her parents took her to Weymouth on a day trip. It was the very day that Woolworth's opened there, and she bought a pair of dogs.

On Sundays, when I was a small child, I was allowed to hold

them, but only while sitting down: at other times they remained in pride of place on top of mum's piano. Mum passed away in 1998, but I still have the dogs, and treasure them.'

Paula Perry

Cheeky costermongers

'I must have been eight or nine years old during the blitz in Catford, South East London.

Woolworth's was on the main road through Catford, and at the back was a bombsite, that had been cleared of all the rubble. The site became a mini 'open market' with lots of different stalls selling their wares. At the time they were known as costermongers. That's where I would earn my pocket money, as parents had no spare money in those days and you had to work for what you wanted. I would work for a chap in my spare time at the market. He had a fruit and vegetable stall with a barrow at the side, which was laid out with different fruits. Sometimes trade would be very slow, so he would push his fruit barrow onto the main road right in front of Woolworth's. He would be doing a good trade and I would be near the doorway of Woolies, keeping an eye out for a policeman. As soon as I saw a copper coming our way, I would give him a nod and he would wheel his barrow back down the side road until the policeman was out of sight. Then we would be back on the main road in front of Woolies again, as that is where all the shoppers were. Woolworth's sold lots of things, including good biscuits and broken ones, but no fruit. It was worth the hassle of moving the barrow.'

Alan Kerry

Huntley and Palmer's

'Broken biscuits were sold from glass-topped tins, with iconic names like Huntley and Palmer emblazoned on them. They were sold by weight and passed to the customer in paper bags. I always preferred these to pre-packaged biscuits, as invariably one would find fragments of cream and chocolate biscuits among the selection.'

Ian McGill

The Frome store, opened in 1929 but unchanged in the 1940s when Derek Phillips remembers being taken there by his mother and bought banana-split toffee from the sweet counter

Slab toffee and the silver hammer

'Around 1946 my parents moved from Yeovil to Frome. As a young schoolboy, one of my main memories of the Frome store was the sweet counter – in particular Palm toffee which was only sold by Woolworth's. This would be in large slabs and was broken up for weighing by the assistant with a small silver hammer. My favourite flavour was banana split and I can still smell and taste the flavour today.'

Derek Phillips

The wonder of Woolco

'After finishing work on Fridays, my family used to travel to Woolco near Bournemouth to do our weekly shopping. The staff were very helpful. Woolco was featured in the Guinness Book of Records for being the first out-of-town shopping centre with the largest floor area, and the very first automatic car wash. Everything was under one roof and, during Christmas, the outdoor area was illuminated with a fountain, which changed colours showing various colours of the rainbow.'

Kevin Hatton

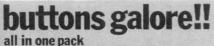

buttons galore!!
all in one pack

winfield
housewife's button pack
SHIRT & PYJAMA BUTTONS

It's well worth shopping at
WOOLWORTH

Picture: author's collection

Bright colours

'At the Woolworth's store in Douglas, Isle of Man, I can remember being lifted up to see the button counter and choosing buttons for a dress my mother was making for me. It was 1946 and I was four years old at the time. I think I asked to see the buttons every time we went there. I vividly remember the bright colours.'

Ruth Wyllie

Real diamonds

'Having returned to Guernsey after the war, aged six, my earliest memory of Woolworth's is of a large building at the bottom of St Peter Port. I distinctly remember the beautiful use of wood, for the floors, counters and all the shelving. Little rubber dolls, around an inch and a half in length, cost thru'pence to sixpence. My sister Anne once remarked to mum that the tea-set two girls were looking at was only 21 shillings. The girls overheard and were much amused: they were obviously not as 'refined' as we were. I also remember that my sisters and I saved up our pocket money to buy mum a birthday present. It was a beautiful crescent-moon brooch costing one shilling and sixpence and containing, as we assured her, real diamonds!'

Daphne Farnham Patrick

Display cabinet is still going strong

'I was a regular Woolies shopper. One purchase I believe is worth a mention was a display cabinet bought from the Hemel Hempstead branch in the early 1970s. In those days, they sold flat-

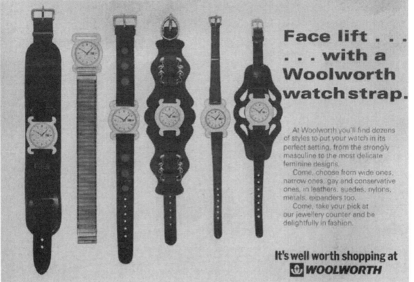

Face lift . . .
. . . with a
Woolworth
watch strap.

At Woolworth you'll find dozens
of styles to put your watch in its
perfect setting, from the strongly
masculine to the most delicate
feminine designs.
    Come, choose from wide ones,
narrow ones, gay and conservative
ones, in leathers, suedes, nylons,
metals, expanders too.
    Come, take your pick at
our jewellery counter and be
delightfully in fashion.

It's well worth shopping at
WOOLWORTH

pack furniture, which some of my acquaintances turned their noses up at, believing it to be of lesser quality than furniture sold at more 'acceptable' stores. That cabinet is still going strong, having survived one house-move and several room-moves. It looks a little dated, but with a glass cabinet, two shelves and a base cupboard, it remains a useful asset in my living room. How much of today's furniture will last for 35 years?'

Sue Bartlett

A poor family's luxury

'We have fond memories of Woolies in South East London, going back to our childhood in the 1930s, when it was the 3d and 6d store. A pair of slippers would cost threepence or sixpence, and there was everything you needed for sewing, knitting, or for mending shoes (a necessity in the days of the Depression). They sold broken biscuits in large tins that resided on the counter, and Alan's mother, who was a widow with four young boys, sent him to buy half a pound, but to ask for whole ones. These biscuits were a great luxury to poor families.'

Joan and Alan Linstead

From Fablon to Canada Dry

'In those pre-refrigerator and freezer days, shopping expeditions took place several times each week, and in my early years I recall that we used to visit Woolworth's in Wimbledon about twice a week. It occupied a corner site at the junction of Gladstone Road and the Broadway, the frontage being on the Broadway.

The fascia proudly announced 'F W Woolworth & Co' and each section had its own staff, till and heavy, dark counters of polished wood on which were displays of toys, confectionery, biscuits, ribbons, buttons and stationery. I also remember as a boy buying gummed strips to make into paper chains at Christmas and, in later years, more modern and sophisticated decorations as well as waxed cardboard plates, drinking straws, serviettes and plastic table covers. At one time they also sold their own records under the name of Embassy, which were chart singles but recorded by artists other then the original singers.

The counter staff, almost invariably female, seemed to me to be in their mid to late teens, and the uniform issue included white headwear with the 'W' symbol emblazoned in red on the front. Rightly or wrongly, Woolies staff in the immediate post-war period were a byword for sloppy and slovenly service, a reputation which persisted, especially amongst the older generation, until the interior of the store was refitted for self-service, and those massive counters were consigned to history.

The flooring was of timber, laid herringbone fashion. Although the shop-floor was lit by electricity, gaslights had also been retained for use in the event of a mains power supply failure (a not uncommon event in the winters of the late 1940s and early 50s). I seem to recall that some at least of those massive gas fittings were permanently illuminated, in a kind of 'belt and braces' situation presumably.

After the Second World War, DIY mania started and in came revolutionary bright colours and easy-clean materials in home décor. Woolworth's began to stock Fablon, which came in a range of bright colours and bold patterns and was displayed in large rolls. The assistant would cut it to your required length and you then just peeled away the backing paper and stuck it down, smoothing

The store in Fore Street, Trowbridge, Wiltshire, opened in 1929 and is seen here around 1973. Another familiar name in the high street – Fine Fare – was next-door

out the wrinkles and air bubbles. It transformed any number of surfaces and brightened up your home.

At the rear of the store was the goods lift, with lattice gates through which a curious child could watch fascinated, as the car and huge counter-balance travelled up and down the shaft.

Woolworth's also sold ice-creams and, on those rare hot summer days of half a century ago and more, my mother would buy us each a cornet. Of course, the ice-creams were not the soft creamy creations of today but simply a deep solid disc, which sat precariously on top of the cornet and required great care in being eaten lest it fell from its tenuous perch.

Later I recall that Canada Dry beverages were available from a special display area, while the advert of pick 'n' mix confectionery meant that the family transferred its allegiance from local sweet shop to Woolworth's. We also bought salted peanuts from a counter where cashew nuts were also sold. Mum bought ribbons by the foot (or yard) from the large reels on which they were displayed, and buttons on cards.

If you couldn't carry everything, you could buy brown paper carrier bags for 2d, though it was always a worry as to whether heavy or sharp items would cause the carrier to give way. In wet weather, of course, they would rapidly give up the fight and in snow, the hapless shopper would be left with just the handles.

When we moved away from London about 40 years ago, my wife and I lived in Bath before moving to Westbury. We frequented the city centre branch of Woolworth's in Bath, on the corner of Stall Street and New Orchard Street, and bought a lot of things for our new home there. The retail area was spread over two floors, with electrical goods, light fittings and tools on the first floor. The ground floor included a café, and during the period when we lived out beyond the Bath Racecourse, we used to go into the City each Saturday morning and would often have lunch at Woolworth's before taking the last bus home at about 3pm.

When we moved again, our nearest Woolworth's were Warminster and Trowbridge and we used to go there to buy CDs and DVDs. Over the years on our travels around the UK we've called in at Woolworth's from Penzance to Caithness. The town of Pembroke Dock in Pembrokeshire, West Wales, boasted a small branch of Woolworth's on the north side of the main shopping street. Running roughly parallel with this thoroughfare was a single-track railway connecting Pembroke Dock Station with the former HM Dockyard about a mile further west, at Paterchurch Point. One very hot day in high summer several years ago, I called in at this branch of Woolworth's to get some confectionery and drinks. Browsing around, I noticed that the doors of the emergency exit at the rear of the ground floor were open, admitting a welcome draught of air. Being of a somewhat inquisitive nature, I resolved to see where this exit led, mindful of the presence of a railway nearby. To my surprise, the emergency exit led out directly on to the right of way occupied by the line to the old dockyard! Current Health and Safety legislators would doubtless have apoplexy at the mere thought of such an arrangement.

Woolworth's was not merely a place to shop but an institution which exuded a permanence such that we couldn't imagine life, or a town, without them, a focal point in smaller communities which arguably held town centres together, an anchor which we fondly imagined would always be there.'

Ian McGill

Picture: Keith Fletcher

The Chesham store in the 1960s, flanked by two other stalwarts of the high street: Millett's clothing and camping shop and Dewhurst's butchers. The Woolworth's window is promoting hairspray at 3s 11d

Shoe repairs

'I remember being taken to our local store in Chesham, Bucks as a child in the 1940s to buy loose sweets whilst my father bought seed potatoes. Later we regularly shopped there especially to buy stick-on soles and rubber heels to do our own shoe repairs.'

Keith Fletcher

An art deco look

'My first experience of Woolworth's was on trips with my parents to the Commercial Road, Portsmouth, branch. When we had finished shopping, dad would take us to the cafeteria which was

A 1960s Woolworth's display of Little Beauty dressed dolls, available in various sizes and all with 'rooted hair'

accessed by a large staircase at the back of the shop. Here we enjoyed a cup of tea looking down onto the main body of the store. I later discovered that this cafeteria floor area was called the 'mezzanine floor'. Suspended from the ceiling was a huge cornice that swept from one side of the cafeteria in a semi-circle and had an art deco appearance.'

Peter Taylor

Broken biscuits for 6d

'We always bought a box of broken biscuits at Woolworth's for 6d – that was in about 1932. Little did I realise I would be working at Woolworth's in later life.'.

Ivy Leonard

Penny in the slot

'I was a regular visitor to Gosport town centre every Friday to look around the lovely shops. It always ended in Woolies, where I had toys and handbags bought for me by my mum and grandmother. One handbag, I recall, had a doll's face on it, and was grey with two handles. They were usually made in Hong Kong and China. Our trip always ended in Paley's, where we had a cake and cup of tea with dad's side of the family before going home on the bus. Also in Woolies was a weighing machine. You put a penny in the slot and got a card out with your weight on one side and a picture of a dog on the other. It was awesome.

When I was five years old and started school, I missed our Friday shopping trips, but after school we'd sometimes go on the Gosport ferry to see my grandmother in Portsmouth. On the way, we'd go to the market, then into Woolies to buy slab cake, water biscuits and sweets for me. We ended our shopping trips by visiting mum's sister, Edith, who worked in Woolworth's selling ice-cream in a cone from a machine. Finally it would be time to board the bus to my grandmother's.

I was seven years old when my brother was born and he also accompanied us on our trips. From the age of 8 to 16, I went on annual school outings: we always took a packed lunch and always went to Woolies to buy souvenirs and a postcard.

My mum and two grandmothers all wore powder, rouge and red lipstick. I was 13 when I became interested in make-up. At the Gosport Woolies they bought Max Factor and Yardley, but I bought Miners because it was cheaper. I had Miners 4 Cream Eyeshadows (green, blue, purple and silver), Miners pale pink lipstick, and orange nail varnish. Lemon face packs were a must

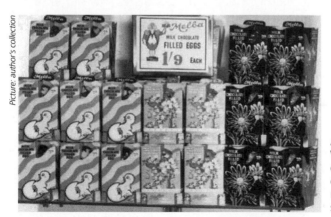

Picture: author's collection

A 1960s Woolworth's display of Melba filled chocolate eggs ranging from sixpence to 3s 3d

and so were sachets of Vosene and Stablond shampoo. I was about 13 or 14 years old when my Auntie Eileen paid for me, herself and a girl I sang with in the school choir, to see Cliff Richard and the Shadows. My dad gave me some money to cover my bus fare and buy a drink during the break – and to buy a ring at 2s 6d from Gosport Woolworth's. I already had a heart-shaped locket from the Portsmouth store, and a watch from my grandmother. The ring was an imitation of a lady's silhouette surrounded by mock Marcasite.

I left school at 16 and went to work in an office, but still did my shopping in Woolies. In the Portsmouth Woolworth's you could buy cardigans and jumpers (they were not sold in the Gosport store). When I got married in 1973 my chief bridesmaid had a car, so I went to Portsmouth Woolworth's and bought a dozen bottles of sparkling wine for the reception. A lot of my wedding presents also came from Woolies.

We moved to Dursley in Gloucestershire, but their small Woolworth's had closed, so we used to visit branches in Stroud, Gloucester and Bristol for our paper chains and Christmas baubles. Even when we were on holiday in Gibraltar in the 1980s we managed to find a Woolies. Alas, they are no more.'

Linda Smart

Top prize

'My mum and I entered a competition in 1978 at the Preston store by estimating the number of sweets or chocolates (from memory, possibly Twix bars) that had been placed in the lid of the record player. The prize was the record player itself. My estimate was closest to the correct number and we were invited to a presentation evening held upstairs in Woolworth's with a buffet provided. A lot of the staff were there too.'

Jennifer Howson

More than just a shop

'When our local Woolworth's was closing, my 26-year-old son came in and said 'people are saying that if you have memories of Woolworth's, don't go in because the place is being torn apart'. He said he could not understand that people would get upset, because it was only a shop. But it was more than that. I have vivid memories of going down town with my siblings to spend our 6d pocket money on a Saturday morning and the wonderful counters all set out.

I remember Christmas time when toys would be hung from above, and I especially remember when our local Woolworth's got its record counter. I have to be honest and say I thought Woolworth's had had its day and I would not miss it: then last week I needed a new button, and today I wanted to buy some new cotton. I had always gone to Woolworth's for these things – you don't know what you have until it's gone.'

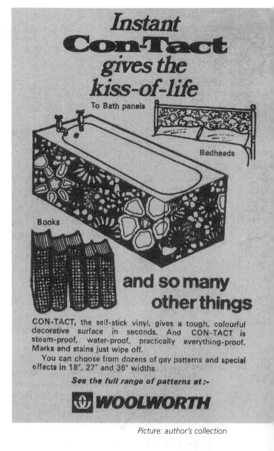

Picture: author's collection

Maureen Graham

Just the pudding, thanks – I'm skint!

'Let's go back 60 years. I worked in Leicester and always went to Woolworth's restaurant for my dinner. The queue went all the way down a side entry, up a flight of stairs, then all the way round the restaurant to the serving area. I would say there were at least 50 people waiting. Depending on how well off I was, I had the main course plus pudding and a cup of tea all for about 2s 6d. At the end of the week I could only afford the pudding. Happy days.'

Audrey Bailey

Picture: author's collection

Shoppers crowd the pavement outside Woolworth's at Gallowtree Gate, Leicester, in 1938

Woolworth's plays cupid

'My friend and I used to go into Woolworth's in Gallowtree Gate, Leicester, every day for dinner and there were some lads who also came in. We got talking to them and one of them, who I quite fancied, asked me out. I went out with him for two years; we married in 1952 and were together for 42 years right up until his death. So I have Woolworth's to thank for meeting my husband.'

Winifred Burton

A lifesaver

'I came to London from Jamaica in the West Indies in 1955, and Woolworth's was my favourite store to shop. There was a very large one in Holloway Road, with one entrance in Holloway Road and the other in Seven Sisters Road. Coming here from the West Indies, we have a different accent and we called some things by a different name, so when we went into some shops they did not know what we wanted. Woolworth's was a lifesaver: you could walk in, see what you wanted, pick it up, and take it to the cashier.

Apart from that, you could find anything that you needed. I used to do a lot of embroidery and we would draw our own designs – in Woolworth's, you could buy them with the drawings already done. The only thing they did not sell was fruit and vegetables. When that store closed, we still had one in Caledonian Road and one at the Archway. Woolworth's will be greatly missed.'

Pearline Williamson

A cure for the homesick

'I have shopped in Woolworth's for many years. For me it is very nostalgic. When I first came from Germany in 1958, at the age of 18, I could speak very little English and felt very homesick. Then I found Woolies.

In my hometown there was a store very similar to Woolworth's, where you could buy the same kind of things —you could just walk through and look. It felt a tiny bit like home.

When I look round my home now, there are so many things that came from Woolworth's: my first electric lawn mower, and the little hooks to hang baubles on the Christmas tree. Kids' clothes, too, and also books, paint, kitchen utensils, knicker elastic, sewing cotton, gifts, tools, toys, music, seeds and even slug killer. The list is endless.

Where will we go now to get pick 'n' mix? On my shopping trips, I often walked through Woolworth's. Recently I went to the shoe mender to get some strong thread to fix my slippers and they said 'go to Woolworth's'. We all miss Woolworth's sorely.'

Gisela Soinne

From Russia with love

'I remember taking a group of Russian school children to the Woolworth's in Edgware Road in April 1990. They were from School 611 in Moscow and it was one of the first ever home-stay exchanges between Russian and British schools. The staff went to great lengths to demonstrate how a Western store operated, by taking the somewhat bemused teenagers from loading bay to warehouse, to shop floor, to checkout. Then, after chocolate and drinks, they were each given a voucher to spend in the store. What

Picture: Ruth Wyllie

Pupils and staff from School 511 in Moscow, on exchange with James Allen's Girls' School, Dulwich, pictured outside Woolworth's flagship store in Edgware Road, London, in April 1990. The chairman of Kingfisher, Sir Geoffrey Mulcahy is third from the right in the back row

fun they had doing this. Some decided very quickly; others wanted to acquire some small souvenir for every member of their family. Perhaps they are now telling their own children about their magic afternoon in Woolies.'

Ruth Wyllie

Walking on air

'My friend loved Woolworth's and wherever we travelled, she never missed visiting a store. Some years ago we were on holiday in London and had spent the day sightseeing. As the day wore on, my feet became more and more painful as my shoes were not suitable for walking far. I was really crippled. When going down one of the main streets on our way to Victoria train station, we passed a Woolworth's store and of course my friend went in. I leaned against a counter feeling very cross at my friend's seeming thoughtlessness for my plight. Very soon she returned carrying a pair of velvet slippers. I think they cost 6/11d. I put them on and was walking on air. How ashamed I was to have misjudged my friend – and how grateful I felt both to her and to Woolworth's.'

Renée Pelan

From Aladdin's cave to army checkpoint

'Gale-force winds and driving rain persuaded me up the steps into Woolworth's. In truth, I was using it as a refuge, but I might just as well buy my chocolate there. I passed through the line of cash desks spread across the entrance like an army checkpoint barrier and on into the shop. My grandma would never believe this to be the Woolworth's she knew, I thought.

I looked around at the narrow alleys between walls of hooks with items hanging and shelves with items standing. What a miserable labyrinth it was and how poor compared with the Woolworth's of a generation ago.

As a London schoolgirl in the wartime 1940s, my friends and I passed our local Woolworth's four times each day. At 4pm on the way home we would go in, entering the store from one side and exiting from the other. It was a veritable Aladdin's cave. It would never have occurred to me in those days to do my shopping anywhere else. Originally a 3d and 6d store, everything was within my financial reach – even if I did sometimes have to save two weeks' pocket money to buy one of the more expensive items.

On entering, one was invariably greeted by the Andrew Sisters singing *The Three Caballeros* or *The Boogie Woogie Bugle Boy from Company B*, while air – thick, warm and scented – assailed one's nostrils.

Stained wooden floorboards, shading pale with wear, ran the length and breath of the store. Rich red mahogany counters stood off the perimeter walls by about three feet, allowing assistants to work behind. The remaining mass of floor space was criss-crossed with wide aisles within which were long rectangular islands of counters. And

Pre-paid telephone cards were introduced into the UK in 1977. This one is a joint promotion by British Telecom and Woolworth's to publicise Mother's Day

running through the centre of these were narrow workways with access points at each end for the assistants. Cash registers were placed every 10 to 15 feet. The top of the counters, fractionally and deliberately too high for small hands, were about four feet deep, with the back slightly higher than the front, providing a gentle slope and elevating items at the rear. It was also separated into compartments by plate glass dividers and it was within these compartments that so much variety lay.

I was always drawn to either the stationery or jewellery counter. Stationery had a rich collection of notebooks, pencils, fountain pens, sharpeners set within a small metal globe of the world, multi-coloured rubber bands and more. On jewellery were all kinds of rings, some with imitation gems. There were signet rings and wedding rings in rolled gold, bracelets and necklaces, small Union Jack brooches coloured with luminous paint, supposedly so that the wearer could be seen in the blackout. The haberdashery department offered a myriad of ribbons from quarter-inch baby ribbon to six-inch wide satin finish. Cards of silk cord, braid and fringes sold by the yard. For men there were socks, elastic arm bands, braces, suspenders, ties and bow ties. For ladies, combs, dinkie clips, alice bands, stockings and garters. For children multi-coloured rubber balls, footballs, cricket bats and marbles.

On another counter one could buy spectacles with metal rims painted to look like tortoiseshell. A printed card with letters that diminished in size enabled one to select the lens with the right magnification. There were briar pipes and pipe cleaners. Loose biscuits were sold by weight from 7lb tins and – if you had coupons – sweets and chocolates. On the walls were rolls of American cloth, which was wipe-clean and used on kitchen tables. This was sold by the yard and also in narrow widths with a fancy edge for shelves. There were paper doilies that were sometimes given to small children to paint, in the hope that the task would keep them quiet, garden tools, paintbrushes, Aspro's, and sticking plaster. The cosmetics included Tangee lipsticks, powder, rouge, Evening in Paris perfume or even Californian Poppy. There were nails and tacks for upholstery, and half-inch wide rexine trim. The list is endless.

There was very little Woolworth's did not sell. Stock control must have been a nightmare but I don't remember anything ever being out of stock and in those days sales records had to be kept by hand in huge ledgers and numerous box files.

The girls' uniform was simple. Assistants wore burgundy red button-through dresses, and supervisors wore royal blue and carried dozens of keys around their waist. Periodically during the day, they would empty the tills of bank notes, carefully recording how much was taken because the cash had to balance. Any shortage had to be made up by the assistant. Supervisors were called when further change was needed and to deal with customer queries. They were considered quite superior and were always smartly turned out. Sloppiness in any form was not allowed.

For youngsters Woolworth's was a meeting place, as servicemen on leave soon discovered. There were always attractive girls to be found one side of the counter or the other. It was easy to watch someone surreptitiously from among the crowds while moving from one section to another – and to skip out of a side door if escape was expedient.

I remember clutching my pennies tightly as I searched for a birthday present for my mother. The household counter attracted me with its array of cotton floor mops, baking tins, china and glass. I suddenly spotted exactly what I wanted. It sat there glistening under the dancing lights, a small glass cream jug on a saucer. It had a diamond moulded into the surface, imitating cut glass. I thought it looked quite expensive. It cost me 4d. Mother's cream jug stood on the dresser for years, a useful receptacle for odd buttons and pins. Jugs like it now turn up at antique fairs, priced at around £8.

I don't know when the change took place. I can't recall seeing it happen, but suddenly the heart had been ripped out, the 'social centre' destroyed to be replaced by boring passages of dull merchandise. Sixty percent of the commodities had disappeared and the atmosphere totally annihilated.

Outside, the rain still lashed and the wind still blew. No snack-bar in this Woolworth's where I might warm myself with a cup of tea. I picked up the chocolate and stood for several minutes queuing at the only cash desk, while someone ahead of me searched for her Access card.'

Sylvia Fortnum

Sixpenny specs

'When my grandma and grandpa were visiting Manchester from Birmingham, he wanted to go to Woolworth's to buy some new spectacles. This would have been around 1930, when I was six years old. Grandma said 'my sight is about like yours, so get me some too'. I went with him. The rows of glasses were on an open counter and, being small, I could just about see them. They cost

Picture: author's collection

Oldham Street in Manchester in 1931, with Woolworth's on the right sixpence a pair and had oval wire frames. He tried them on and read a card to check they were OK. He then bought two pairs.'

Josephine Deacon

Magic-painting books introduced me to art

'I was born in 1928 and can remember when I was old enough (about five or six) I went to stay with my grandma. She would take me with her on the local bus to Market Harborough, Leicestershire, to do her weekly Tuesday market-day shopping. My favourite shop was Woolworth's. I could not wait to see the counter with the magic painting books, coloured pencils, crayons and paint boxes. I had to stand on tiptoe to see everything and to choose what I wanted to buy. My grandma would impress on me not to reach out and touch anything or I might be asked to buy it, but to point to whatever I wanted to the assistant behind the counter. I did so look forward to these visits. On looking back over my life, I sometimes wonder whether these visits to Woolworth's with my grandma were what inspired and encouraged me to become an amateur painter with a great love of art.'

Cynthia Deakin

Copying America

'I used to say to my daughters, Rebecca and Phillippa, that if they didn't get good results at school they would be serving behind the counter at Woolworth's. This was an indication that you start at the very bottom.

At the Market Harborough branch, Dorothy Smith was the manager. The shop had counters that sloped down and the assistant stood behind to serve. In the centre of the floor, the counters would be round all four sides and the assistant would stand in the middle. That store was up the High Street, opposite the Old Town Hall. In more recent times Woolworth's moved down to The Square.

I used to cycle to Market Harborough in the 1950s and 60s to catch the train, and this was the opportunity to go into Woolies to buy what I needed to finish the clothes I was making. Woolworth's sold everything you needed for your home sewing, usually press-studs, zips, cottons and needles.

When I worked at English Electric in Rugby I used to go to town to buy the records of the day at Woolworth's. I also liked their pick 'n' mix sweets, and the whole range of chocolates that were sold much cheaper than elsewhere. I used to buy Ladybird clothes for the children – they were cheaper and more modern for that particular time. They also sold leather soles for mending shoes.

The demise of Woolworth's began some years ago, when we copied America with the idea of supermarkets. At first it was just a handful, but later came the out-of-town shopping stores.'

Rachel Root

Bobbies, double-deckers and Woolies

'My first visit to the UK from France was in 1968 when I was a student. I was 18 years old and spent my summer holiday with a family in Cornwall, as a paying guest. I took pictures of everything which seemed to me to be typically English, including bobbies and double-decker buses. This was in case I might not visit again, and I wanted to fill up an album with all of my wonderful memories: Woolworth's was one of my favourite haunts, mostly for sweets. I loved Cornwall so much that I returned every summer and eventually met the Englishman who would become my husband. I hitchhiked just about everywhere with newly made friends; something young people cannot safely do any longer. I am still in touch with the lovely family I stayed with that year. 40 years on, I have now been living in England for nearly 38 years.'

Daniele Skinner

A two-bob bit

'I was living in Taunton during the mid 1950s and I clearly remember Woolworth's selling Phul Nana and California Poppy perfumes. The names and smells made a big impression. I can also still picture myself buying a set of stamps on the occasion of Grace Kelly's wedding, and a brooch for Mothering Sunday. It was mother-of-pearl 'look-a-like' and the word 'Mother' was written in gold-coloured wire. One Easter I remember a chocolate egg with an inset 'scene' edged with raised frilly icing; and on one visit I found a two-bob bit on the floor (I have been looking down ever since). I also remember the paper bags of broken biscuits: it was often the only way you got to taste the cream and chocolate ones. My married sister bought bacon and cheese on Saturday afternoons from non-refrigerated open counters and I clearly remember us taking the bacon back one time as it had not been protected from flies —with the obvious consequences.'

Susan Benling

The day Tommy Handley died

'On Sunday 9 January 1949, a nasty sleety day, I was in Woolworth's in Yeovil when I heard someone say that Tommy Handley had died. Tommy was a great comedian, whose radio show ITMA – *It's That Man Again* – kept the nation laughing through the dark war years and into the years of austerity that followed. This was quite a blow to an 11-year-old whose main source of radio comedy was ITMA.

One of my other great enthusiasms at the time was American comics, but they were like gold dust. They were not at all like the British comics such as the Beano or Dandy which were basically just funny, but were full of adventure, very highly coloured, printed on reasonably good paper with lots of pages and with characters such as Superman, Captain Marvel, and detectives of the like of

Picture: author's collection

Hardly the image of the 'swinging 60s' — a display of jumpers from 1965

Dick Tracy. Hundreds had been handed out by the American GIs when they were stationed in and around Yeovil during the war. However, around 1947 American-style Classic Comics began to be sold in Woolworth's and I think this was the only shop in Yeovil which stocked them. The comics were based on classic books and I can remember buying *Westward Ho!* and *Lorna Doone*.'

Jack Sweet

Scared off

'On leaving the Grass Royal Secondary Modern Mixed School at the age of 14, I started to look for a job. Firstly I had an interview at Woolworth's in Yeovil for a starting position of trainee stockroom assistant. I vaguely recall being amazed at the range, extent and variety of goods. I was quickly scared off when it was emphasised that I would be required to memorise everything and its location. A visit to the Junior Labour Exchange set me up with a job as office boy at Bradfords Coal Merchants in Hendford at 10 shillings per week.'

Derek Rogers

Picture: author's collection

everybody's sweet thought

Milady *toffees...*

FOR TASTE QUALITY & VALUE
The sweets you're always sure of selling

MANUFACTURED BY WALLER & HARTLEY LTD., BLACKPOOL

Peppermint? Yuk!

'Our local Woolworth's in Croydon sold cordials in all flavours and you could have them hot or cold. At six years old, I longed to try the red ones, but my mother insisted on the peppermint flavour, which I did not like. After the war was over, we came to Yeovil and when we entered Woolworth's there was a lovely smell of roast peanuts, usually near the door. There was also music playing from the record department, adding to the atmosphere. I can remember visiting the cafeteria with my mother and young brother on Saturdays for tea and buns: my brother said he had something in his eye and an American GI said it must be a currant.'

Eleanor Pugsley

Hayricks, beware

'It must have been about 1936 when (shock, horror! The town would go to the dogs!) Woolworth's opened in Walton-on-Thames. It was, of course, a huge success, especially for us children who loved just walking round it. We lived in Esher Avenue and it was quite a hop into town. My brother and I were given 2d a week pocket money, which we spent on Fry's chocolate cream bars. Later, at about the age of 12, we bought pipes and cigarettes – the latter for stuffing into the pipes, which we smoked out in the fields until Farmer Dunell saw what we were up to and, fearing for his hayricks, shooed us away. We had a poor-as-a-church-mouse governess, dear Miss Duncan, who bought us Easter eggs in Woolworth's which she could not afford and which must be the most treasured presents I have ever received. Woolies was not just another shop: it was a way of life and a store of memories.'

Daphne M F Byrne

Rolling pin lasts 70 years

'I was engaged to be married in 1938 and purchased, from the Wells branch of Woolworth's, a rolling pin costing 6d, six sherry glasses at 6d each, and six half-pint glasses at 6d each. Only two of the half-pint glasses remain, but the other articles are still in use today.'

Nancy Kingston

Furry cuddles

'Mum had four children under 10 years, and took us to Woolies in Ilkeston, Derbyshire, so she could do her shopping. This was in the 1950s. At that time, fur coats were very fashionable, and I loved to cuddle them. I was the second eldest and should have known better: I'd been told to mind my younger brother and sister, instead of grabbing any woman's fur coat as she passed by. There I was among a mass of cuddly fur, saying 'nice'. I clung on for dear life, ignoring all the turmoil it caused to mum – and to the cuddly coat owner. I also re-member during my childhood enjoying lucky bags from Woolies, and sherbet lemons with the liquorice stick. The lucky bags cost 3d and contained a 'treat', a tiny plastic toy. I still like fur, artificial of course, but have never owned a fur coat.'

Denise Smith

My very own Jacko

'As a small child in the early 1950s I used to love the toy counter in Woolworth's. I had a monkey on a stick, jointed and made of plastic, which climbed up and over the stick when you pushed the handle up. I also bought a traditional-looking little wooden horse standing on a green base with red wheels. I think it cost 2s 11d, but lasted throughout my childhood. I called it my Wooden Horse of Troy.

The toy I really wanted was a Jacko monkey, which was actually a toy chimp. In the summer of my fourth birthday, I had been taken to London Zoo and loved the monkeys and apes, but especially the chimpanzees. I desperately wanted one of my own. In Woolworth's there were these wonderful toy ones, hanging by their bendable hands on high railings. I spent many months saving my sixpences until I had the grand sum of 22s 6d.

Picture: Helen Meyrick

Going to buy Jacko was surely one of the most exciting shopping expeditions of my life. He was made of flimsy material and stuffed with straw. His hands, face and shoes were made of soft plastic. He was not made to last, but was very loved.'

Helen Meyrick and her sister Jill pictured in the 1950s. Helen is holding Jacko the monkey, which she bought at the Eastbourne store after saving her pocket money for many weeks

Helen Meyrick

Sheet music was very popular in the early years of the twentieth century. Many homes had pianos, but people also bought the music so they could sing the words, or even just whistle the tune. Sales were phenomenal and in one 12-month period the Woolworth stores in the US alone sold 20,000,000 copies of sheet music at ten cents a copy, this price being much cheaper than anyone else's. At all stores, including the ones in the UK, there would be a counter displaying the popular tunes and ballads of the day. A piano was positioned nearby, and if requested, an assistant would play any piece of music the customer was interested in. The shopper would hand over sixpence for their copy of the sheet music and depart satisfied.

Play it again, Wynn

'My wife's mother worked as a pianist and vocalist at the store in Exeter way back in the 1920s. Winnie worked under the name of Miss Wynn Andrews and it was her job to play and sing the pieces requested by customers before they bought the sheet music. It was often a great gathering-place on a late Saturday afternoon for the Exeter and district young people and in fact it was the way my parents met. Dad, Bill Derges, was one of those 'potential customers' and they married in 1926.'

Ian and Mary Creek

Dance while you work

'When I first started at the Erdington store in Birmingham, records were sold and the top ten was played and my friend and I used to dance to the music behind the counters.'

Gail Ashton

A catalogue issued by Woolworth's in July 1932 advertising their Eclipse Records range: 8-inch shellac records selling at 6d each. A glimpse through the catalogue at the vocal section gives us such gems as *Don't Tax the Working Man's Beer* and *He Played his Ukulele as the Ship Went Down*

No more fuddy-duddies

'On a Saturday when Newcastle United were home we would go up to the match but the next Saturday when they were away we would buy a record in the store and spend the evening listening to it. It was great when they opened the record counter as the only other shop selling records in town was owned by what we thought was an old 'fuddy-duddy'. Then all of a sudden, girls of our own age in Woolies were selling records and we could discuss the latest hits with them.'

Lila Walker

Word for word

'Many moons ago I worked in Woolworth's in Oxford Street, London, during my summer holidays. I was on the record counter when Frank Ifield's *I Remember You* was Number 1 for 28 weeks. In those days Woolworth's did not sell records by the original artists, but people bought the song on the Embassy label and didn't worry about who was singing it. I sold hundreds of copies of that single and knew the whole song word for word because I played it so often. After a while I went upstairs into the cheese-packing department. In those days Woolworth's sold cold meats, cheese and other food items. I cut up cheese, weighed it, shrink-wrapped it, priced it and, as a consequence, didn't eat cheese for a few years after that.

I did enjoy my short time at Woolworth's and remember it fondly. Everyone was very friendly but the only name I can remember is a Miss Mussell who lived in South Kensington. It was over 46 years ago but I still remember my time there and it is very firmly implanted in my mind and always will be.

In January 2009 I went into Woolworth's in Fareham, Hampshire, to see what they had left. What a sorry state it was in – it so upset me I had to leave without buying anything. What had gone so horribly wrong here? It didn't feel right to see the shelves empty and the store selling off the shelving, tables and chairs. In fact it broke my heart: none of our high streets will ever be the same again without that familiar name. The Woolworth's around here still have the name proudly standing out but there is nothing inside.'

Elaine Emery

Tie Me Kangaroo Down, Sport

'I still have in my possession four Embassy records namely:
    Rikki Henderson – *It's Now or Never/Save The Last Dance*
    Paul Rich – *Tell Laura I Love Her/Lorelei*
    Buddy Stevens – *A Mess of Blues/Tie Me Kangaroo Down Sport*
    Johnny Worth – *Ginger Bread/Western Movies*
When I look back at the titles I wonder what possessed me to buy them. Was it the price?

They were only five shillings. It was over 50 years ago, so it's rather a long time to remember.'

Maureen Forsyth

Abba takes me back

'I was a 15-year-old Saturday girl in Woolworth's, Luton, in 1974. It was my first proper Saturday job and it was a very new and modern store having relocated from the High Street to the newly built Arndale Shopping Centre Complex, with Woolworth's being one of the first stores to open. I started in the haberdashery department but my overriding memory was working on the record counter just after Abba had won the Eurovision Song Contest with *Waterloo*. I remember I had to play this song every other record! I must have played it over 40 times during my shift. Even today when I hear the song, it takes me back to Woolworth's and those seventies times.'

Anna Jones

'While shopping in Woolies with my grandmother in Richmond, Surrey, at around the age of 10, she offered to buy me a record for playing on the new Dansette record player I was given for my birthday. I chose *Volare* by Paul Rich and I think I played it to death. My interest in Embassy records having been fired up, I used to travel into Richmond on my bicycle each Saturday to buy one or two of the latest hits. It probably depended how much I had left from my paper-round and school dinner-money. I lived in East Sheen and although they had a large Woolies there, it did not sell records.

I left school at 16 and went straight into an electrical engineering apprenticeship. One of our first jobs was to put three-phase electricity into Oriole's new studios in New Bond Street and help install some of the equipment. I was in Seventh Heaven when I found out that Oriole made Embassy records, and I spent a long lunch-hour telling (or probably boring) a senior executive about my collection. In those days I had a reasonable voice with a good range and when I told him this, he said I could sing backing vocals on a song 'for posterity'. I did this one Thursday afternoon and it must have been quite successful as he said I could 'have another bash'. I'm not sure of the first one, but the second was *Bobby's Girl* sung by Kay Barry. Her real name was Barbara Kay and she had been a singer in the Oscar Rabin Band. From then on, I sang backing vocals at the studios about once a month until 1964.'

Brian Robinson

★★★

The origins of easy-listening music in Woolworth's go back to the 1920s when Little Marvel, a record label owned by the Vocalion record company, was sold exclusively by Woolworth's from 1921 to 1928, retailing for 6d – well under half the price of Decca and HMV records sold by Woolworth's competitors.

Also introduced into Woolworth's in 1921 was the Mimosa label, owned by Crystalate, which featured a 5½-inch single-sided disc. By 1928, this had been replaced by the Victory label. Like the Little Marvel, it was sold for 6d and was a 7-inch record which played for around 2.5 minutes and ran at 78rpm. Victory, in its turn, was replaced in 1931 by Eclipse: many of the most popular stars and dance bands of the era appeared on the label including Harry Leader and his band, Leslie Sarony, and Cavan O'Connor. Inflation – or lack of it – can be judged from the fact that even in 1935, Woolworth's still managed to keep the price of a record at the same level as in 1921 – sixpence.

During the 1930s, Woolworth's equipped each store with a gramophone and sales of records soared: music was played constantly and Woolies became the most popular place to buy records.

Embassy Records, produced and manufactured by Oriole Records, appeared in November 1954 and were sold exclusively through Woolworth's. At the beginning they were 10-inch 78rpm records, but were eventually replaced by 'singles', the seven-inch 45rpm format which became the standard across the industry. These double-sided releases featured cover versions of current hits and traditional tunes recorded by session artists – usually big-band musicians and singers recording under a pseudonym. Speed and cost was of the essence. The skill was to predict which new song or instrumental would get into the charts and then record a cover version, producing it so that it was ready for sale the following week. The recordings were made, usually on a Thursday, at Levy's Sound Studios in Mayfair, London, owned by Oriole Records bosses Jacques and Morris Levy. An average of 30 minutes was allowed for the recording of an individual song, and up to four different songs would be completed over four hours. Artists were paid a one-off fee for their performance and did not receive royalty payments. The records were then manufactured by Oriole in their plant at Aston Clinton and distributed to all Woolworth's stores by the following Monday ready for sale. Embassy records ran very successfully for 11 years, ceasing production in 1965 when Oriole was taken over by CBS. This was not the end of the association with Woolworth's, however, as CBS launched the Hallmark/Pickwick Top of the Pops series of albums, long-playing 33rpm records containing 10 to 20 tracks. No artistes were ever identified on the labels, although it is well known that Elton John recorded for the label.

Eventually, Woolworth's entered the branded market of records and later with CDs, remaining the leading UK music retailer well into the 1990s, and easily outselling competitors such as Virgin Megastore and HMV until severe competition from cost-cutting supermarket giants such as Tesco and Asda made serious inroads into sales.

Picture: author's collection

Love and Marriage – but not by Frank Sinatra. The Embassy record label, sold exclusively through Woolworth's, released cover-versions of popular music

Vocal gems EP from The Merry Widow, released on Embassy and featuring the Embassy Light Opera Company

Picture: Brian Robinson

Frankie and Johnny, Steamboat Bill and four other tracks from The Coffee Bar Skifflers on this EP on the Embassy label. The sleeve-notes promote the music as having 'all the sparkle of a night out in the town's gayest rendezvous – the coffee bar'

Picture: Brian Robinson

A compilation of old favourites including *For Me and My Girl*, *If You Knew Susie* and *Don't Dilly Dally on the Way*. The Embassy sleeve-notes for this EP point out that music is the perfect means of getting your party under way, along with 'the drinks flowing nicely, the cigarette smoke curling up to the ceiling'

PARTY TIME

LILY OF LAGUNA
PACK UP YOUR TROUBLES
IF YOU WERE THE ONLY GIRL IN THE WORLD
AINT SHE SWEET
IF YOU KNEW SUSIE
ANOTHER LITTLE DRINK

Picture: Brian Robinson

Embassy HIGH-FIDELITY 45 RPM

EXTENDED PLAY   FULL-RANGE

Holiday in Spain

The sleeve-notes for this Embassy EP describe the *Spanish Gypsy Dance*, *Granada* and *La Paloma* as the 'music of a sun-scorched land. Music to set your blood afire'

Picture: Brian Robinson

PAPER CHAINS AND FAIRY LIGHTS

CHRISTMAS AT WOOLWORTH'S

At one time, there was no other store to be in than Woolworth's at Christmas, with crowds of shoppers pushing and jostling, and customers shouting at the hard-pressed shopgirls that they were next to be served. Festive music – usually Jingle Bells *and* White Christmas *– blared out from the record department and the counters were piled high with toys, dolls, jigsaw puzzles, crackers and Christmas decorations.*

Shouting the odds

'I worked as a Saturday girl at Woolworth's in 1956 on the tills at Hawthorne Road, Kingstanding, Birmingham. The manager was a big burly man and he singled me out to sell on the 'Christmas line' which was a separate counter at the front of the store. He grabbed a box of Christmas crackers and said to me 'come on, Missy, shout the odds like this', waving a box of crackers in the air and shouting to the customers 'roll up, get your Christmas crackers, excellent value' and then pushed the box into my hand. I took a very deep breath and, shaking in my shoes, repeated what he had said. He insisted that I shout louder and wave the box more. My second attempt was much better and, as the customers took note and started picking up the crackers, I got into the spirit and happily adapted my own theme and we cleared quite a few boxes. I was given a free cup of tea and a slice of toast at break time, courtesy of the manager.'

Hazel Booth

I've still got my Christmas tree

'When I was a little girl in the 1960s, my mother Ethel Phillips worked in the Yeovil branch at Christmas. She worked on various counters including the sweet counter where there was a hot container for the very popular peanuts. They were good days, but mum had to work hard. I remember my nanny Mrs Neil taking me to see mum on a Saturday, and I had to wait outside because I was not allowed to go into the store before she had finished. The manager, Mr Beddows, was a strapping man with a smart suit and polished shoes. All the staff respected him, but one day he threw an apple across mum's ears as it was not good enough to sell. In those days, the store sold everything from fresh fruit to DIY. On the toy counter, one of the most popular toys was a monkey with hanging arms which went very well: it was put into brown paper bags and kept behind the counter until collection.

I'll retain these memories for as long as I live. I still get great satisfaction from having known every single counter in the Yeovil branch and I find it very sad that the greatest store ever has closed for good. I think revamping the store was Woolworth's first mistake. I miss the Yeovil store and particularly the Sherborne branch, which was the best one and always will be. Bring back the old Woolworth's and the employees – I say this for my mum and my two brothers as well as for myself. Incidentally, I still have the Christmas tree that mum bought at Yeovil Woolworth's for 65p in the 1970s and I use it every Christmas.'

Carole Watts

Choosing our presents

'My mum Ethel Phillips always worked in Woolworth's at Christmas time to bring in extra money to help keep us, as dad had died some years previously. We, that is my sister Carole and my brother Derek, were allowed to pick something out as a Christmas present, and (lo and behold!) on Christmas day there it was. The old Woolworth's stores were nice, with their dark flooring and gas lamps with wired glass shades. The staff in their uniforms were always polite and helpful. On a Saturday I would go into the Woolworth store in Yeovil with my sister to get some of their fruit cake, with strict orders from mum to tell who ever served us that we did not want the end piece. Mum used to come home tired out after being on her feet all day, and would then start cooking tea for us all. They were hard days in the late 1950s and early 60s when people like the Woolworth staff worked for far less than today's minimum wage, but in many ways I think they were far better days.'

Nigel Phillips

Jigsaw was top present

'In the build-up to Christmas in the 1940s and 1950s the Frome store would be packed out. All of the staff were behind large wooden counters each with a large cash till. One day my brother, my father and I were at the jigsaw puzzle counter which was piled high with puzzles of all kinds and remember my father buying us a lovely jigsaw puzzle of an American Steam locomotive.'

Derek Phillips

Glitter added value

'If some Christmas cards did not sell, the manager at the Above Bargate store in Southampton got the girls to trace the outline shapes of the people and buildings with glue, then sprinkle the card with glitter to make them more attractive, increase the price and boost sales.'

Harold Gilham

Bells regulated our day

'I remember working for Woolworth's as a Christmas temp in December 1934, shortly before my 18th birthday. My first job at the Commercial Road store in Portsmouth Hampshire was on the calendar counter, which was obviously busy because of the season.

As a result of my efforts my contract was made into full-time, although I must admit I came close to being dismissed on a couple occasions because my lifelong good-natured cheekiness got the better of me with the manager, Mr Page, and his under-manager, Mr Potter. My reply to criticism remains to this day: 'I couldn't give a monkey's'. As was the norm in the pre-war years, work itself was conducted in a very strict and disciplined manner. Before we were even offered employment our home circumstances had to be investigated. With the exception of widows, single female staff were expected to be living with their parents in a good environment with good character references.

Once you had a job, you had to be measured for a tailor-made Woolworth's uniform. The company recovered the cost with weekly deductions from wages. Daily routine seemed to be governed by bells. We were expected to be on the premises by 8.40am on workdays and have to hand over our handbags for security reasons and then change into our uniforms. All jewellery and stockings were banned on the retail area. At the sound of the first bell of the day we had to file to our allotted counter and prepare for opening time. At 9am a second bell rang to indicate that the doors were open for trade.

I used to get a one-hour lunch at about 11.30am. When I first began the job I used to run home, eat the meal prepared by my mother, and then run back for the afternoon shift. When my mother became pregnant with my brother I was given permission to eat in the Woolworth's canteen, where I soon got sick to death of a regular diet of steak and kidney pies. The afternoon included a statutory 10-minute break for tea but otherwise it was a long shift at the counter. In the evening another bell would sound to give the customers warning that trading would soon end; once all the customers had gone the fourth bell would ring.

But that wasn't the end of the bells. A fifth would indicate that staff should place a fire bucket behind their counter (there were no sprinkler systems in those days). The next indicated that tills should be opened for clearing by the supervisors, and only when that was complete did the final bell sound to indicate that we could leave our counter and return to the staff room to end the shift.

A particular feature that I remember about pre-war Woolworth's was the extent of personal service to customers. We would for example, receive unadorned chocolate Easter eggs which we had to decorate to the individual customer's requirements, including wrapping and ribbons. We would also apply the required trimmings to lampshades that arrived at the store in a basic range of materials and colours.

Picture: Getty Images

Christmas rush in a London Woolworth's store on 1 November 1955

In those days, as was normal, the store closed on Wednesday afternoons. On Christmas Eve, however, it was open until 10pm because the festive buying season culminated with everyone rushing around at the last minute to complete their shopping for the holiday. No months of Christmas promotions and sales then! On top of the late night before Christmas, we all had to return to the store early after the break to do a personal stock-take, right down to the last nut and bolt if you happened to be in the hardware department. On those occasions we all pulled together to help each other, which was another nice feature of the Commercial Road store.

We had a social club on Southsea seafront where we had regular dances and other get-togethers. It was probably this mix of hard work and a good social interaction with the other staff that saved me from the sack when my humorous side got the better of me.

I left Commercial Road in 1938 on my marriage to Ernest, who unfortunately died from injuries sustained while serving with the NAAFI on board HMS Ark Royal when she sank in the Mediterranean as a result of enemy action. When war broke out in 1939 I returned to the Commercial Road store but bombing later destroyed it. I was then called up for war service as a laundress at HMS Victory. My final stint with Woolworth's was also rather brief, as smaller premises in the North End area of Portsmouth had replaced the Commercial Road store. I went there in early 1946, but left at the end of the year when I re-married.

Looking back on those days, I would say that the experience at Woolworth's was a happy and rewarding one with a firm where my managers stood by the motto 'the customer is always right.'

Marjorie Stephens

All my presents for sixpence

'In about 1933–1934, living on the South Coast, I was given 6d before Christmas to do my Christmas shopping for the family: my mother, father and sister. I bought a mirror for 2d, a comb for 2d and pad and pencil for 2d. Remarkable!'

Betty Donaldson

Pram made it a special Christmas

'My first experience of visiting a Woolworth's store was at Christmas 1965 when I was seven years old and living in Portsmouth. I went with my mum, dad and brother to visit the toy counter at the North End branch, and my parents bought me a doll's pram which cost them £8. I was very pleased to receive this pram. As the years went by and I became a teenager, I used to buy nearly all of my pop records at Woolworth's since 7-inch singles would only cost about 65p.

One of my favourite memories of this store was that they also sold electric chord organs made by Bontempi or Rosedale. The organs would have a notice on them saying 'please play me' to encourage people to try before buying. At 14 years old I was, and still am to this day, a rather keen musician and so could not resist trying one out. I was spotted playing the organ in the store by my dentist who complimented me on how well I played – a surprise to me as I had only played a piano before. They also had organs at the larger branch of Woolworth's in Portsmouth's Commercial Road, but the public could only try them out if they played 'properly'.

When I left school at 16 I took a series of temporary jobs and one of these was at Portsmouth's third branch of Woolworth's in Palmerston Road, Southsea. I worked on the toy counter and enjoyed it very much. They also sold electric organs and very occasionally I would entertain the other staff.'

Loredana Walsh

Christmas tree takes a walk

'One Christmas when I was working at Woolworth's in Broadmead, Bristol, we had a large Christmas tree on display. It was at the rear of the store near the window and there was a waist-high barrier around it. On the Saturday the store was heaving with people with no room to move. Staff suddenly noticed the Christmas tree proceeding down the store held above the heads of the people. We assumed display staff were moving it to the other end of the store. Later we discovered someone had stolen it – they had just climbed over the barrier and taken it, carrying it through the store and out of the Broadmead entrance. Staff could never understand why they had carried it the whole length of the store and not just gone out the door next to the display area where it was on show. It caused much amusement'.

Cathy Howard

Stock-taking time

'After Christmas in the Twickenham store, the annual stock-take took place and I can remember being sent to one of the DIY counters to count endless sections containing screws and nails which were sold individually. Every single one had to be counted.'

Carol Anelay

What a squash!

'I was born in 1949 and my earliest memory was as a three-year-old being taken to Woolworth's in Gosport, Hampshire. It was Christmas time and I was squashed up against a counter by women including my mum and grandmother. They were scrabbling to pick Christmas cards as they had glitter on them and were only 6d each. We also bought paper chains and fairies to pin on the wall.

Picture: Getty Images

Christmas shoppers crowd to buy novelties and decorations at Woolworth's store on Oxford Street, London on 14 December 1937. The goods were piled high on the counter and the customers allowed to rummage through them

That Christmas I awoke in my parent's bedroom and saw a stocking hanging up, with an orange and some nuts in it. We lived with dad's mum and her brother Uncle Walter. It was Uncle Walter who carried me downstairs to open my presents. At tea time that evening we had a cracker each (which were bought in Woolies). In Uncle Walter's cracker was the cardboard head of a North American Indian with a cigarette in his mouth. Uncle Walter set the cigarette end alight and the Indian was smoking.'

Linda Smart

Saving up

'The Christmas goods would arrive at the stockroom at Didcot in August. I remember my first Christmas present for my parents was a complete set of crockery consisting of cups, saucers, tea and dinner plates, which I bought on a weekly basis and hid at home until the day.'

Ann McKinley

Christmas – and baby – comes early

'In December 1982, I was Christmas shopping in Woolworth's Sutton Coldfield, when half way down the escalator I realised that I was experiencing early labour pains. My third child had decided to come early. I managed to get home safely and then went to hospital that evening and Heather was born just after midnight. Afterwards, every time I used that escalator I thought of that happy day.'

Elizabeth Wolsey

It was Foil Magic

'The Christmas ranges at Redhill, in Dept 29, were fabulous, particularly the imported tree decorations from Europe. I clearly remember serving the new tinsel ranges one afternoon in mid-December from an eight-foot end-display, with one assistant just taking the money and keeping the display full. We sold boxes and boxes of the Foil Magic twist-hanging decorations, and the sales racked up by Dept 19 with its fantastic range of cards, calendars and diaries, was just unbelievable.'

Alan Munn

Pocket money presents

'Woolies was the first and only 'port of call' in Yeovil for Christmas presents. The hobbies record-book I kept as a schoolboy records my Christmas present purchases for myself, parents and close relatives: this was probably around 1934 or 1935 and it all came out of my weekly pocket money of 6d. For myself, an imitation pistol at 1s 6d, a torch at 1s 3d, and three darts for sevenpence ha'penny. For dad, a handkerchief and a pipe rack at 1s 1d; for mum kitchen scales at 5 shillings; for grandma soap at one-and-six; for my aunt a toaster at one-and-six; for my uncle a sixpenny pack of cigarettes, and for my friend an egg timer at a shilling.'

Derek Rogers

And mother came too

'One Christmas in the Croydon store before the war, they had something I had never seen before or since. There was a Father and Mother Christmas in a little cottage and they seemed like a real couple and so nice.'

Eleanor Pugsley

Picture: Graham Rowe

The Penzance manager plays Father Christmas to Cheshire Home residents

Picture: Graham Rowe

Helping residents of the nearby Cheshire Home with their Christmas shopping at the Penzance store after closing-time

Woolies plays host

'Patients from the Cheshire Home would come to buy their Christmas shopping at the Penzance store after we closed and the staff gave up their free time to help them as much as they could, giving them cups of tea and snacks. The store manager would dress up as Father Christmas and give a present to each of the patients, which we all got for them, and they all went home happy. This made our Christmas.'

Graham Rowe

A real Christmas

'I remember finishing work at the Sutton Coldfield store one Saturday just before Christmas and my feet were killing me because we had been really busy. I walked to South Parade in the dark, to catch the bus home to Falcon Lodge and it began to snow. I had been selling selection-boxes all day and the combination of selling Christmas goods and the heavy falling snow made me feel really Christmassy. It was a real traditional Christmas, which I will always look back on longingly.'

Sue Cooke

Evening in Paris

'I remember at Christmas I would go to Woolworth's at Cosham, Portsmouth, with my brother and sister to buy Christmas presents for my parents and uncle. It was always the same gift every year as we didn't have lots of money to spend: a sixpenny hankie for my dad and uncle, a bottle of Evening in Paris for my mum; and an autograph book for my sister, I can't remember what I gave my brother.'

Anita Hancock

Christmas romance

'It was in 1950, when I was just 16 years of age, that I started work at Woolies as a Christmas extra in the store at London Road, Portsmouth. On Christmas Eve, I was told that I was being kept on. Working in the storeroom was a blond chap of twenty-one. And by the end of January 1951 we were going out together. In those days staff were not allowed to go out together: it meant the sack. We were not found out until November 1951 when Dennis was told he had to go, unless he gave up seeing me. They offered him a transfer to another store that was miles away from where we lived, but he said no. He had worked there for almost eight years. I begged the manager to sack me instead, but he said the rules were that the male had to go. So I had a job and he didn't. The story ends happily: we have been married 56 years, with a wonderful daughter and son, five super grandchildren and three wonderful great-grandchildren. So we both say 'thanks Woolies', we would never have our family if I had not gone to work as a Christmas extra.'

Gladys and Dennis Hopwood

Picture: Kevin Higgins

The Winter Sweets counter in 1960 at the Northumberland Street store, Newcastle-upon-Tyne. Behind the counter is Kitty Higgins

WOOLIES AT WAR

WOOLIES AT WAR

It was a busy lunchtime on Saturday 25 November 1944 and New Cross Road in Deptford, South East London, was teeming with people hoping to find a bargain. Everything was on ration and mostly hard to obtain, but this did not stop the eternal optimism of the Londoner. It was bright and dry, and the light snow of earlier in the week had melted from the pavements. Many of the shoppers were heading to Woolworth's, on the corner of Goodwood Road and New Cross road next to a branch of the London Co-operative Society. Word had spread that Woolies had received a rare supply of tin saucepans, a scarce commodity in wartime when all available metal was being placed into the war effort to build aircraft and vehicles.

Housewives, children, pensioners and servicemen jostled for service, hoping to pick up not just a saucepan or two but maybe a small something towards Christmas. Queues were a daily feature of wartime Britain – just along the street there was a queue outside a draper's, and another at the fishmongers. Staff from the nearby Southern Railway station at New Cross noticed them when they popped into Woolworth's for a cup of Bovril during their lunch-break.

They had barely taken their first sip when, at 12.26pm, a German V2 rocket containing 2,000 lbs of high explosive slammed into the roof of Woolworth's at approximately 1,000 miles per hour. A brilliant flash of light and a tremendous explosion was followed by a momentary silence before the walls bowed and the entire building imploded and disintegrated. So great was the force of the

Picture: Ron Weston

Gilbert Oscar Weston lived in the house behind Woolworth's in New Cross, Deptford. A retired Southern Railway engine driver, he was one of the victims of the V2 rocket attack on 25 November 1944

explosion that the whole of the store was thrown into the basement. The bodies of shoppers and members of staff were buried under tons of masonry and twisted steel girders.

Next door, the London Co-operative Society was also destroyed. Clouds of dust and smoke billowed from the devastated site, bodies were strewn everywhere, and bricks, masonry and tiles rained down from the sky. Where the Woolworth's building once stood, there was simply a massive gap with the acrid smell of cordite hanging in the air.

Passers-by were caught up in the explosion too, their bodies thrown for great distances and strewn along the pavements and roadway. Even several hundred yards away, people were physically pushed backwards by the blast and felt the hot air from the explosion blow against their faces. A military lorry had been overturned and all the occupants killed; trams and buses had been hit including a double decker that had spun around in the road. Every occupant of this bus was dead, the passengers still sitting in their seats, covered in dust from the explosion. A woman found her husband's van, crushed like a concertina: she never did find his body. Amid the billowing smoke could be heard the sound of screaming from the injured. The trail of devastation stretched all the way from the Town Hall to New Cross Gate station. Official figures record the losses as 168 dead, including 15 children, and 122 injured. It was the worst tragedy in the whole V2 campaign in London and one of the worst civilian disasters during the Second World War. One of the witnesses of the explosion, Robert Ball, disputes the official figures: he describes the explosion as sounding like an earthquake and the subsequent scene, with 'arms, legs and bodies spread out over a very wide area' as being horrific. 'Bodies were placed into Vestry Vans (dustcarts) by the score during the day', he said. 'We estimated over 1,000 casualties, but the government at the time censored it just to keep morale up'.

Within minutes of the attack, the rescue squads were at work; brick by brick the debris was removed by hand in the hunt for bodies or survivors. It was to take three days for local people and the emergency services to hand-sift through the rubble of what had once been a Woolworth's store. Around 80 bodies were recovered from Woolworth's alone, many of them children, still clasping the toys bought for them.

A replacement Woolworth's store did not appear at New Cross Road until 1960: there were strong rumours that the building was haunted. A plaque on the building, now occupied by an Iceland store, was erected by Lewisham Council and Woolworth's to commemorate the people killed on that tragic day, the youngest of whom was a one-month-old baby and the oldest an 80-year-old man.

The Nazi rocket programme was developed by a team of scientists led by Major Wernher Von Braun, a top-ranking SS officer. Unlike the earlier V1 rockets which flew relatively slowly at low altitude, the V2s Vergeltungswaffe 2 (Reprisal Weapon 2) were a very sophisticated weapon and the world's first ballistic missile. Measuring approximately 14 metres tall with a circumference of 1.6 metres, they were each equipped with a warhead containing 2,000 lbs of high explosive. They had a range of 225 miles.

One single V2 was capable of destroying an entire street of houses, arriving without warning at the speed of sound. Propelled by a liquid fuel engine the V2, from its launch in Northern France and other sites in Belgium and Holland, would ascend 52 miles in 60 seconds before the engine shut down and the missile would then fall to its target by the pull of gravity, reaching a closing speed of 1,000 mph upon impact.

The V1 was a 'doodlebug' and could be heard coming, with its engine spluttering until it cut out, before diving and exploding. The V2 was silent, deadly and fearsome bringing morale to an all-time low to Londoners, thousands of whom were living in the icy days of winter in houses devoid of glass in their windows, roofs without tiles – that is if they had a roof at all – and no running water.

For seven months Greater London bore the brunt of casualties and damage: around 500 V2 rockets were dropped on London between September 1944 and March 1945 killing 2,754 people and injuring 6,476. A large proportion of the 1,050 V2s fired against our country during the war fell short or went wide, mainly in Essex, Kent and Hertfordshire.

★★★

Keep calm and carry on

'One day during the Second World War, at the height of the blitz of Southampton, my mother decided to risk a trip into town with the hopes of buying much needed items. Rationing was having a severe affect and most of the daily news came by word of mouth as the whole country was in a state of secrecy. So what would our shopping trip produce? Not much as we arrived to find a high street full of rubble, and no sign of Woolworth's! At the original entrance stood a man with a placard. He directed the few customers across a wide ditch via a builder's plank. and down we went into the cellar of Woolies. Some trestle tables had been erected with an assistant at each and for light a hurricane lamp had been placed on each table casting many shadows to show the few undamaged goods available for purchase. Not a very successful shopping trip and that night another air raid! On our heads we wore saucepans for protection against shrapnel.'

Sheila Hunter

Picture: Imperial War Museum

In Plymouth, Woolworth's was destroyed in an air-raid and the company opened a temporary shop in the market. This picture is from October 1941

Woolworth's escapes bomb

'During the War the Westland Aircraft Works in Yeovil was an obvious target for the German Luftwaffe, but apart from one attack in March 1941, when several employees were killed, the Works suffered little damage: all the bombs fell around the factory or in the town.

The first raid on Yeovil took place just before 4pm on Monday 7 October 1940. In just a few minutes, high explosive and oil-fire bombs rained death and destruction across the town. A direct hit demolished an air-raid shelter at the Vicarage Street Methodist Church, leaving four housewives dead and over 30 people injured. In Middle Street a bomb exploded between Montague Burton's shop and Woolworth's, killing eight people who had been sheltering in the shop or in the billiard room above. Montague Burton's premises were demolished, but miraculously Woolworth's, together with the 200 or so people sheltering in the shop, was undamaged.'

Jack Sweet

Firewatching – to music

'At the Clayton Street store in Newcastle upon Tyne, staff would act as 'fire watchers' during the war. It was part voluntary and part compulsory. You'd work for two nights in the shop with a water pump and a bucket of sand at the ready, in case of firebombs. We never had a fire when I was there, but to while away the evenings, we would play records on one of the gramophones for sale, and dance up and down the aisles to the music of Deanna Durbin. I worked at Clayton Street from 1940 to 1942, when I left to join the Land Army.'

Winifred Mullen

Shop was a lifesaver

'Woolworth's saved the life of a young Wimbledon woman during the Second World War,. It was the mother of a school-mate of mine: she was shopping in The Broadway when a German fighter plane flew low over the area and opened fire on the road. A passer-by dragged her into Woolworth's – an act which almost certainly saved her life.'

Ian McGill

Picture: National Maritime Museum.

Nothing left: the ruins of Woolworth's after the V2 strike of 25 November 1944

RISE AND FALL – A TIMELINE

1852   Frank Winfield Woolworth is born on 13 April in Rodman, New York

1873   Starts his first job at a dry-goods store in Watertown, New York

1879   The first Woolworth's five-cent stores open in Utica, New York and Lancaster, Pennsylvania

1886   Seven Woolworth's stores are now in operation in the US each of them displaying the carmine-red shopfronts

1890   Frank Woolworth makes his first buying trip to Europe

1900   Annual sales reach five million dollars

1905   The 120 stores are incorporated as F W Woolworth & Co with Frank as President

1909   The first British store opens in Liverpool

1912   Frank Woolworth amalgamates his US stores with the five-and-dime stores run by his brother and cousin, giving him a total of 558 stores in the US, 32 in Canada, and 12 in Great Britain

1913   The Woolworth building, the tallest skyscraper in the world, opens in New York

1919   Frank Woolworth dies on 8 April aged 66 leaving a retail empire of 1,081 stores

1920   Palitoy (then called the Cascalloid Company of Leicester produces its first toy, a windmill, and sells through Woolworth's

1921   The 100th store in the UK opens, in Mansfield Nottinghamshire

1925   Town councils inundate the company with requests for a Woolworth's in their area

1931   The British company floats on the London Stock Exchange

1932   The trading partnership with Ladybird begins with Woolworth's UK placing an order for 96,000 units of ladies underwear

1935   Upper price limits for Woolworth's goods in the US and UK are abolished

1944   V2 rocket kills 168 people at the Woolworth's in New Cross Road, Deptford

1951   Woolworth's becomes the premier memorabilia store for the Festival of Britain

1952   The stores stock a two-shilling Airfix kit of Sir Francis Drake's ship – the Golden Hind – sold in a plastic bag in order to keep costs down. Huge sales of models of all types through Woolworth's will make Airfix a market leader

1953   Woolworth's becomes the leading stores for Coronation mementoes with its range of mugs, plates, bunting and gold foil crowns. One million models of the Coronation state coach, made by Lesney Products, are sold during the year

1954	Embassy records is launched, featuring cover versions of current hits sold exclusively through Woolworth's
1955	The first self-service store opens in Cobham, Surrey
1959	The Golden Jubilee of Woolworth's in Great Britain with 1,028 stores in operation and 89 percent of all goods still sold for five shillings or less. Woolworth's moves to a new head office in Marylebone Road, London
1960	Woolworth's worldwide annual sasles top one billion dollars
1963	The Winfield brand name is launched
1969	The store in Briggate, Leeds, is damaged by a major fire
1970	Woolworth's starts a store closure programme, shutting 15 stores a year, to fund the purchase of B&Q, a chain of DIY outlets
1974	The store in Bangor, County Down, Northern Ireland is badly damaged by a terrorist attack
1975	'The Wonder of Woolworth's' TV advertising campaign is launched, featuring Jimmy Young, Tony Blackburn and Henry Cooper with music by Georgie Fame
1979	Fire at the Manchester store claims 10 lives
1979	According to theGuinness Book of World Records Woolworth's is now the largest department storechain in the world
1982	Links with the US parent company are cut as the British stores are sold to Paternoster Stores Ltd, later known as Kingfisher
1984	Woolworth's buys the exclusive rights to the Ladybird name from Coats Viyella
1986	Woolworth's buys its toy and games supplier, Chad Valley
1993	The closure of half the US stores is announced
1994	Most of the stores in Canada are sold to Wal-Mart
1997	The last 700 Woolworth's stores in the US are closed: the company changes its name to Venator
2001	The US company changes names again, this time to Foot Locker
2001	Woolworth's in the UK de-merges from the Kingfisher Group and is floated on the London Stock Exchange
2006	The 'Big Red Book', designed to be a competitor to the Argos catalogue, is launched
2007	The 'Worthit' brand is released: advertising campaigns featuring Worth the dog, Wooly the sheep and celebrities such as Rolf Harris and Kelly Osbourne
2008	Woolworth's goes into administration, closing 815 stores with the loss of 30,000 jobs. The last stores close on 6 January 2009
2009	Former manageress Claire Robertson reopens the Dorchester, Dorset, store under the Wellworths name.